EXCHANGE

Anecdotes of an American Host Family and Their Foreign Exchange Student

Hannah Overly

En Pointe Publications

Exchange

En Pointe Publications

ISBN-13: 978-0-692-16641-3

Cover art: Matthew Smith

www.529books.com
Cover and interior book design

AFS

AFS, formerly the American Field Service, boasts of being a leader in international exchange programs in more than ninety countries for more than sixty-five years. Its mission is: "To work toward a more just and peaceful world by providing international and intercultural learning experiences."

Volunteer host families are asked to provide students with a bed, meals, and the same care they give to their own family members.

INTRODUCTION

Although significant time has passed since hosting our exchange student, Rafael, the trials and tribulations come up as if they happened yesterday. Our year together will remain etched in my family's minds forever. A day seldom goes by without mentioning Rafael, accompanied by some humorous anecdote.

In recounting our Rafael memories with family and friends, using lively hand gestures along with associated vocal intonations, our stories frequently evoke a range of reactions. By the end of many stories, we've broken into gut-busting, snorting laughter with our audience often breathing a thank-God-it's-you-and-not-me sigh of relief. Appreciating the breadth and novelty of our experiences, many then urged me to write about our "Rafael Stories." I want my family, Rafael included, to have a hard-copy memento of our journey for when memory fails.

All humor aside, our stories also convey the challenges of opening our home to a stranger. Though possibly a deterrent for some, that is not my intent for sharing. Although I cannot recommend a host experience for everyone, I can say the rewards have been more than I ever imagined. The laughter and feel-good moments with Rafael have balanced out any struggles we faced. During almost a full year together, we sailed through the highs and submarined through the lows. Where my mantra, "treat him like my own" complicated some matters, it was that mental foundation that committed us to invest in this process—an engaged approach abundant with varying colors, including the wonderful grays that life can bring as no situation is ever really black or white.

Our year with AFS provided us with the invaluable life lessons of tolerance, commitment, acceptance, understanding, and self-reflection. The relationship we formed with Rafael created a new dimension in our Overly family story, one that continues to impact each of us. Plus, we've learned to confront and solve problems and acknowledge that authentic relationships form from effort. Was it stressful sometimes? Absolutely, but that is what cemented our entire host year: working through the nuances of everyday life, forming the bonds we continue to share.

We went into this adventure blissfully ignorant. We could have researched more, read more, asked more; but, in a way, I'm glad we didn't. We figured things out as we went, discovering communication as a key tool. We did it our way and, fortunately for us, it worked. The word "exchange" means something entirely different to us now, something deeper, something richer.

In bringing this book to life, a friend suggested I alter the sequence of events, to more evenly distribute some of the rockier moments, to encourage a more palatable read. I obliged sparingly. Other than a few minor shifts in sequence, the following anecdotes are, in fact, as accurate as memory serves. A drastic change in chronology would betray the truth of our journey. So, in my attempt to depict a transparent account of how our host experience unfolded, my request to readers is this: Do as we did. Buckle up for the ride—an often-bumpy one—and stay on board the journey until the end. The redemption is worth it.

These are our stories, our exchange. They reflect all we gave and all we received—and then some.

Exchange

1

The Reference

It was July of 2013, and as I was perusing my emails, one in particular caught my eye. Having been a stay-at-home mother for fourteen years, my messages were usually comprised of notifications involving our kids' activities. Instantly, I recognized the novelty of this specific email and it piqued my curiosity. The subject line read: *AFS Intercultural Programs. Reference request for Alysa Smith—your input needed.* I opened it up and continued to read.

Apparently, our neighbors next door, the Smiths, had submitted my name to be used as a reference in their application to host a foreign exchange student. *Cool,* I thought. I'd always had a desire to host an individual from another country, so I was interested to see what the process entailed.

I typed away on my iPad, answering questions about the Smiths, as I sipped my morning coffee. I elaborated on their qualities, notably their strong faith and work ethic, hopefully painting the picture of an ideal host family. As I approached the end of the reference form, I checked off a box indicating I would welcome learning more about this organization's exchange program. Within hours of submitting it, my cell phone rang.

"Hi, I'm Susan Brown with AFS."

Her title, Massachusetts Bay Team Development Specialist, was lost on me. Simply put, one of her job duties required the identification of possible host families who would be willing to accommodate a foreign exchange student in their home. The mere fact that this phone call followed on the heels of my reference submission highlighted AFS's desperation and urgency. A significant number of student applicants had yet to be matched with a volunteer host family, and the deadline was looming. In my moment of do-good, sympathetic vulnerability, I began asking questions.

"Do we get to pick the student?"

"Who pays for everything?"

"How long does the student stay?"

After peppering Susan with inquiries and receiving answers that did not deter me, I hung up and found myself more intrigued by the prospect of serving as a host family. My brain went into overdrive: four kids instead of three, different sleeping arrangements, a "stranger" tagging along during family vacations—the montage in my head played like an endless reel.

What do you think of us hosting an exchange student? I texted my husband, Frank.

He texted back without pause: *WTF?*

In attempting to pacify, I called him at work.

"You know how crazy our lives are already with three kids. Think about it, this kid will be with us for everything. Everything. For how long?"

"A semester. Or year," I nonchalantly said.

"A *year*?"

His words resonated. *What was I getting myself into? Maybe I was biting off more than I could chew. Be careful what you wish for....* Every thought mirrored a classic cliché.

Due to some unknown force, I pressed on.

"Come on. I know it might be hard, but it will be a neat experience for the kids. It will teach them sacrifice and compromise. They'll get to learn about a different culture. And, in the end, maybe they'll form a life-long relationship."

True to form, my husband's practical-but-necessary side emerged. "Who pays for everything?"

Downplaying any details that might signal a red flag, I lobbied.

"The kids still have to agree to it, you know," he relented.

Step one: Husband. Check.

3

A Teenage Mutant Ninja Turtle

Still floored by my husband's soft approval, I decided to move forward. Next on the list: the kids.

Later that day, when Alex, Zach, and Emma congregated in the kitchen, I seized the opportunity.

"I have a question for the three of you. What do you think of us hosting a foreign exchange student?"

A short volley of questions and answers ensued:

"For how long?"

"From where?"

"Will we get a boy or girl?" Emma wanted a girl.

"Where will they sleep?"

Almost instantaneously, Alex (our eldest), volunteered to relinquish his room. *1 down, 2 to go*. Zach, our middle child, was hesitant—"Nah, that'd be weird." Emma, our only daughter and the youngest, was on the fence. I can't even recall the exact points of debate in that conversation, but before I knew it, all three kids gave their stamp of approval.

After notifying AFS our family was on board, the kids and I eagerly reviewed the provided bios of the unassigned exchange students:

Decha, 16, from Thailand:

Decha is a lively, confident young man. He comes from a close family that often takes weekend trips together. He loves both playing and watching sports, especially soccer and basketball. In his free time, he enjoys reading historical books. He is the leader of his school's public speaking club, which has won contests and debates. He would like to study law.

Riku, 15, from Japan:

Riku is a kind and friendly boy who loves to stay active! He practices Kyudo, traditional archery, and serves as manager of his school's club. He enjoys playing soccer, volleyball, and baseball. He is very interested in American culture and loves watching American movies. He is excited to share his Japanese culture with his new family and friends!

Rafael, 15, from Paraguay:

Rafael was born in Brazil but has lived in Paraguay since he was nine. He is a pleasant, disciplined, and happy young man. He is dedicated to his studies and gets good grades. Outside of school, he plays tennis and soccer, and he likes to work out. He also enjoys video games, reading books, and watching TV. He is close to his family and enjoys traveling with them.

There were roughly ten students to choose from. It felt like a weird game—deciding on one student at the expense of another, based on what? A few words? After skimming the broad but brief descriptions, I suggested we select a boy. As these exchange students were of high school age, it just made sense to me. Alex would be entering his sophomore year and could hopefully take the student under his wing.

After much deliberation, we narrowed our final decision down to two. The boy of Asian descent with a fondness for archery, versus the one from Paraguay whose interests paralleled our boys'.

"I think we should go with Rafael," I concluded, after rereading his bio which suggested a family and faith commonality.

"Just like the Teenage Mutant Ninja Turtle. Except spelled with an 'F,' not 'PH,'" one of the kids said.

And so there it was...Rafael.

4

Details, Details

All told, there was only about a month between my initial introduction to AFS and Rafael's arrival. The days filled up quickly as we made preparations and performed required tasks—submitting the application, references and pictures of our house, Rafael's future bedroom, and us; engaging in ongoing correspondences with Rafael and his family; moving many of Alex's belongings into Zach's room (our boys were going to share a room for the duration of the exchange); and buying items both necessary and inviting to welcome Rafael into his new American home. Despite two family vacations in that short period, all that needed to be accomplished was completed.

We researched Paraguay to equip ourselves with partial knowledge of Rafael's home country and culture. What we didn't take into consideration at the time was the fact that, although he lived in Paraguay, he was actually of Brazilian heritage with remarkable allegiance.

As Rafael's arrival date neared, all five of us became increasingly excited and curious. When I first proposed hosting a student to Frank and the kids, the question of "*how long?*" topped the list. According to Susan Brown, we could house Rafael for a minimum of a semester, or for the brave-hearted, a full year. We opted for the semester accommodation (with the possibility of extending through the year), making this endeavor more easily digestible. Of course, should this undertaking prove to be disastrous, AFS offered to, in a worst-case scenario, relocate the student into another host family's home at any point during the exchange. For me, this was out of the question. In my mind, this commitment was like a marriage—only in dire, extreme circumstances would I throw in the towel. For better or for worse.

5 Make No Assumptions

After resolving how long our family would agree to host Rafael, we pondered what he would be like. A summarized biographical capsule cannot possibly depict every nuance about someone's personality. We were all in a discovery phase, attempting to piece together bits of information, making him whole in our minds.

Once Rafael's paperwork was received by the high school, I eagerly drove there to gather as much information as possible. The principal shared a copy of Rafael's application, complete with more in-depth questionnaires about his academics and personal life, including individual and family pictures.

Sitting in my car in the school parking lot, I visually inhaled the application's contents. What additional facts I read about Rafael suggested that he'd be compatible with our family. His academic background, as evidenced by his most recent grades, painted him as a dedicated student. He reiterated that his outside interests included soccer, tennis, and spending time with family. He was not a picky eater, he was organized, he had a dog, and one of his primary goals of committing to an exchange program was to improve his English. The irony in reading these "facts" was not the actual truth behind them. Rather, it was my interpretation that triggered certain expectations.

Avid soccer player....

Physically active, teenage boy....

High-achieving, independent, outgoing, and adventure-seeking....

Family-oriented, Catholic....

In my mind, this was Rafael. However, these inferences belied the full truth and failed to embody the Rafael we grew to know. My simplistic, faulty translation of mere words on paper prevented me from approaching this experience with an unbiased, open mind. In hindsight, I recognize this was only a natural response, making assumptions based on limited information. Though words can be truthful, they can also be misleading.

Many of the pictures showed a family of four, inclusive of the pet—a small, white dog named Floppy that Rafael was loosely cradling. They looked like a happy, close-knit family, and I mentally commended them for embarking on this brave opportunity. I couldn't imagine allowing one of my kids to go to a foreign country at that age without a parent, without me. It's heart-wrenching enough to imagine them leaving for college; why shorten our time together? Did Rafael's parents want him to become more worldly?

Improve his English? Experience a life vastly different than his own?

Whatever their reasons, they obviously valued this mixed bag of new life experiences. How his mother could bear to part with him for that length of time was courageous and admirable to me.

6 A Phil-Am Family

Throughout my childhood, I was always one of the few students in school who checked off "Pacific Islander" on any form requiring one's ethnic background. Considering the range of ethnicities that label included, it seemed so vague and overgeneralized. Nowadays, the choice selection is more specific, while the irony is that many people are of mixed heritage, where "other" seems to be the most appropriate option.

I was born in the Philippines, and Frank was born in Pennsylvania with mostly German roots. His original red hair used to incorrectly suggest a strong Irish influence, but his graying through the years now currently draws numerous Anderson Cooper comparisons. Phil-Am we would be called, short for Filipino-American. Our kids have inherited a blend of our physical features. Hair: not black, not red, but brownish. Skin: not "tan" (as my Caucasian friends call it), not fair, but somewhere in the middle.

Possibly their hallmark feature, hinting at their interracial lineage, is their freckles. The combination, Asian-y with freckles, throws people, prompting the all-too-often question: "What are you?" Appearances aside, Alex, Zach, and Emma also display traits of Frank and me in terms of personality, disposition, intelligence, and physical abilities. We have raised them with a blend of each of our upbringings' influences in regard to traditions, religion, and general lifestyle. And because I have always been proud of our family and any good we can offer, I was confident to welcome Rafael into our Phil-Am world.

7

And Then There Were Six....

We were making the trek from Rhode Island to a Boston suburb to pick up Rafael. The hypnotic effect of raindrops hitting the car did not seem to quell our nerves. As we navigated our way through traffic, I imagined that, in just a few short hours, our lives would drastically change. Even the seating arrangement in our car would be different. The last row of seats in the SUV, which were commonly laid flat, making room for loads of cargo—school backpacks, stench-drenched soccer bags, ballet accessories, groceries, and occasional trash from a fast-food run—would be upright. I could envision the inevitable bickering brought on by forcing one of the kids to sit in a sub-optimal, cramped, motion-sickness-inducing rear seat. I tried to not let that thought or Mother Nature "dampen" the anticipation of our first meeting.

As host families began to filter into the parking lot of our designated pick-up location, I watched them scramble to unload themselves and their belongings. Most everyone carried some sort of welcoming paraphernalia—a sign, balloons, gifts, etc. Of course, my kids were embarrassed that I covered our sign with a garbage bag. I prided myself in being organized, and, at that moment, was grateful to have a layer of plastic protecting the paint, glue, marker, and ribbon on my *Welcome, Rafael!* banner.

We were directed into a lecture hall, which was filling up quickly with host family members, many including children of various ages. Some, however, presented as elderly couples, empty nest syndrome likely fueling their volunteer endeavors. We took a row of seats immediately in front of the Smiths and exchanged nervous pleasantries. Finally, a voice boomed over the crowd, attempting to silence everyone so the introductory AFS meeting could begin. While listening to general information about the program, its local key contact personnel, and praise for our participation, I just wanted to fast forward to our student/family introduction. I imagine most of the audience's thoughts echoed the same sentiment, *Where is our student, and when will we meet?*

Frank, sitting by my side, appeared to be less consumed by the mystery of our first encounter with Rafael. Glancing at his watch repeatedly, his main concern was getting to work on time. Punctuality topped the list of fundamental requirements.

Climbing over and past our legs in the auditorium seating, Frank made a beeline for the closest AFS representative. Pleading about his time constraints to this stranger, he motioned to us to follow him. My next vivid memory is one of our family being ushered ahead of the eager crowd and into a darkened stairwell, dimmed by the absence of natural sunlight. Standing on the landing, I had a straight line of vision through the sidelight windows abutting a door to the foyer below. Like a scene from the Disney movie *A Bug's Life*, the sight of students filing in through the door from the rain reminded me of worker ants walking in a single line with a sense of duty and purpose. I could detect a range of emotions on many of the students' faces—from sheer and giddy exuberance, to a vacant numbness—a no-way-to-turn-back-now realization.

I spotted Rafael among the crowd almost immediately. He appeared dazed and in shock. To look at the bunch, they could have passed for a cluster of American students. To hear them was a different story. Accents, both familiar and unknown, dotted the air and confirmed that these weren't just any students; they were foreign exchange students. And one was ours.

With mother-hen instinct, I pointed at Rafael repeatedly. The gesture seemed to work as his gaze zeroed in on our family. We scrambled through the sea of students for a frantic first introduction, sharing names and quick hugs with one another, followed by a mass exit from the stairwell.

It was the first day of the next eleven months of our new lives. My maternal abacus needed to recalibrate quickly. Because, now, we were a family of six.

Riding back toward Rhode Island, Emma purposely seated in the third row alone, I surveyed everyone's position—Rafael at our car's core, flanked by both of our boys. I could sense the awkwardness between them, their bodies miles apart.

To alleviate some of the silence, I asked Rafael basic ice-breakers: *How was your flight? How do you feel? Did you eat anything?* I attempted to gauge the extent of his English-speaking skills, but my real desire was to familiarize ourselves with each other and re-establish a comfortable dynamic within our family.

By this time, an email from Rafael's mother, Leslie, showed up in my inbox. Translated into broken English from Portuguese, Leslie's message expressed concern regarding his whereabouts and safety. Like tracking a FedEx package with much anticipation, she wanted to ensure Rafael had arrived at his destination. Mother to mother, I wasted no time emailing her from my phone, comforting her with the knowledge that her son was accounted for and in good hands.

8

Welcome to Our World

Prior to Rafael's arrival in the US, he had been residing in Paraguay for several years. Seemingly for the greater opportunities, his parents relocated there from their beloved Brazil. They opened and operated a textile store in Asunción, primarily managed by his mother since his father returned to Brazil for weeks at a time for construction work. Proving to be a financial boon, Rafael's family chose to remain in Paraguay and make it their transient home. From conversations, we deduced that Rafael's parents were able to provide a very comfortable life for him and his sister, Giovanna. Hearing about their vacations, hired drivers, and fine dining experiences, our family appreciated that his parents worked hard and could reap the rewards.

What we discerned early on was that the AFS students all came from means. The kids in the program, by and large, were accustomed to the finer things in life. Their generously comfortable and convenient upbringings disserved many of us host families because we were unaware of, naïve, or ignorant about how skewed socioeconomic differences might influence our thoughts, words, and actions. Had both sides (host families and students) been more educated going into the exchange, perhaps an increased cognizance would have fostered a greater foresight and sensitivity for all.

Based on the casual things Rafael said at the beginning of our journey, such as, "It's not uncommon to spend a couple of hundred dollars on dinner for four of us," and "Usually I come home from school and play video games until bedtime," Frank and I knew that his growth, and ours, would be tested when asked to entertain our family's customary rules, attitudes, and practices. We were from two different worlds, literally and figuratively. We were the adults, he was the child. We were his American parents, he was our Brazilian son. Our respective lives and households manifested in different standards and expectations, both material and immaterial. But Rafael was here in our country because this was the American life he requested.

9 Eyes Wide Shut

In all situations, multiple perspectives exist. The very nature of introducing different cultures into an experience exposes very definitive and contrasting viewpoints. I am certain Rafael's version of our time together would often contradict ours. Not necessarily in the facts, but rather, in the interpretation of and resulting emotions surrounding any particular event.

In hearing stories about other exchange students and their host family dynamics (there were two others in our neighborhood alone, a total of five in our town), the vast variations in host-parenting approaches became obvious. Some served as glorified entertainment coordinators with seemingly minimal rules, which included the responsibilities and restrictions imposed on the student. Though I was cognizant of providing Rafael with numerous enjoyable opportunities, experiences, and trips, the expectation was for him to live as a true member of our household.

This included the same guidance, guidelines, and contributions asked of Alex, Zach, and Emma.

Have you ever heard the expression "tiger mother"? Some take offense to it—the stereotype of the demanding, strict, and rigid Asian mother. Whether the name connotes negative imagery, which it usually does, I admit to being a watered-down version of one. I am strict, I have expectations, and I want my kids to be productive members of society. The directive: "You will be at the top of your class, play an instrument, and be the best," is not an uncommon utterance for many Asian parents. I don't believe I necessarily grew up with that external pressure, at least not in its entirety; my pressure was internally-driven, an innate facet of my personality that fueled self-motivation.

If you ask my children, answering truthfully, they'd say, yes, I display some traits of a tiger mother. Mostly, this is because my style of parenting tends to appear more restrictive and expectant, compared to what they observe at their friends' households. However, I also believe that they have come to appreciate age-appropriate successes, that, in part, are due to my persistent, prodding ways.

Parenting, as Frank and I have come to discover, can be as challenging as you make it. I often remind Alex, Zach, and Emma that it's exhausting for parents to continually reinforce healthy boundaries and rules. "I just want my child to be happy," is a sentiment I hear frequently, but one with which I don't align. Though my children's happiness is very important, my methods of what I believe achieves deeper, more satisfying, long-term happiness differs from that of my fellow parents. Perhaps this was part of the reason why I thought opening our home to a young, foreign stranger might grow each of us in unique, lasting, and intangible ways.

I parent the only way I know how, based on a combination of my own upbringing and each of my children's different personalities. I parent relevant to situations as they are presented. Always a dynamic process, with adjustments made as necessary, Frank and I attempt to make self-analysis a constant piece of the parenting puzzle. It is very much a trial and error exercise, a mental marathon requiring stamina. Above everything, my maternal commandments center around common concepts that are, at times, difficult to enforce: *Be kind, be respectful, and be a good person. Think of others. Be helpful. Be aware—aware of situations where you can help without being asked. Make good choices.*

In the interest of trying to recognize my children's true abilities and skillsets, I make "demands"; I set high standards, for myself and them. Above all, I wholeheartedly believe it is one's work ethic that shapes and directs one's life path and the subsequent opportunities that present themselves. I repeatedly implore my kids to recognize and value the connection between effort and achievement. This said, I also fully acknowledge the importance of balance in life, regarding all aspects. So, where their childhood is concerned, I appreciate the necessity of unstructured downtime, especially in this *overly* (no pun intended) regimented, highly-driven, often pushed-to-the-brink society in which we live. My frequent urging to "get some fresh air" (i.e., play outside) echoes through the house daily. In this technologically-addicted world, nothing frustrates me more than excessive relaxation, time spent on anything with a screen, at least on a beautiful day. I cringe to think that playtime automatically equates to the flip of a power-on switch for today's youth. The unspoken rule for my kids is: "Play hard, work harder."

As for Frank, our parenting styles generally run parallel. He is the breadwinner and, therefore, entrusts me to hold the reins of parenthood firmly in my grasp, tightening, loosening, or steering them as I see fit. Granted, on larger issues where clarity is required, Frank remains a steady, logical sounding board and a presence to offer support, bolster a position, run interference, and moderate conflict. However, on the mundane issues, I parent solo as a stay-at-home mother. It is in my job description, it is the lifestyle we fell into naturally, and I hope that at the end of the day the fruits of my "nagging" will be evidenced in three well-balanced children. I hope they find their passions, strive for a greater good, and experience life defined by their priorities for achieving success. Those are my most sincere wishes, tiger mother or not.

This was the "house mom" Rafael was about to get to know. My methods and belief system seemed to work just fine up until that point and I assumed I could fold Rafael into the mix without issue, even though I had no idea if his upbringing was similar. I hoped the influence we'd have on him would be positive and one that would impact him through his lifetime. As his American mother, I wanted to be a source of lessons learned to partake in creating indelible memories. True to my nature, I was subconsciously putting a lot of pressure on myself and the family in general. After all, we'd only had a few nice photos and words on paper about Rafael to go on when we'd chosen him. Time would tell....

I embraced my role as an AFS host parent as dutifully as possible, and probably adhered too closely to the written word. Many others would claim my approach lent to many frustrations, that if I had "let things go," then maybe the process would've been smoother. Often, Frank would say, "Why are you trying to change him?" Changing Rafael wasn't my goal, but I frequently recalled the "What if it were my kid?" foundation from which to base my parenting style. From keeping his things organized to cleaning his room, to discouraging sexist or racially charged comments, I asked the same of him as my own children. Rafael's responses and behaviors were easily and objectively noted. He either did something or he did not. What I couldn't measure, though, were his thoughts. Did he resent me for asking things of him that he didn't agree with? Most likely, but that was typical of my kids, as well. However, in general, Alex, Zach, and Emma had always been comparably dutiful, obeying what was asked of them as if their eyes were closed and they trusted us to follow our lead. Funny, I thought Rafael could just fall right in step.

10

One of These Is Not Like the Other

Dining out on the weekends ranks high on my list as a priority when allotting my weekly budget. It's rarely a fancy meal for our family, but rather, the typical family-friendly chain restaurant that anchors our time together. The running joke is that I'm a "self-proclaimed good eater." Friends have lamented that I'm the only one who works out at the gym and heads straight to a drive-through window afterwards. Terrible, I know. And though I love a great salad, that is usually the appetizer to a hearty meal, not the actual meal. And I never forget to leave room for dessert.

Our first restaurant meal together as a family of six was on the way home from our introductory meeting at the Massachusetts college. Unsure about what kind of food Rafael liked, we headed to a Chinese buffet. The variety and quantity felt like a safe bet; he could surely satisfy any hunger. He returned from the countless rows of chafing servers with only pizza on his plate. Either he wasn't hungry, or he was unfamiliar with the selection. Regardless, I sympathized he must have felt out of sorts after a day's worth of travel, landing in a foreign country with a new family, and now having us watch his every move. Maybe eating was the last thing on his mind. Eventually, he agreed to finish off his pizza with a novel dessert, an ice cream sandwich from the buffet's freezer. It was comforting to see him enjoy it, and entertaining to watch him manipulate it with a knife and fork.

See, this isn't so bad....

During our second meal out, at Olive Garden, the kids and I stayed true to our chosen dishes and ballpark price point. Unbeknownst to me, Rafael was doing the same—based off *his* lifestyle. However, relative to our family's M.O., his selection of a shrimp dish ruffled me. Even Alex, Zach, and Emma appeared bug-eyed, inherently appreciating the price differential between their entrée selections and his. *Treat him like my own.* Easier said than done.

"I just love shrimp. I don't eat it much back home," Rafael excitedly declared.

Part of me, the maternal side, just wanted him to eat and enjoy it. The other part, the treat-him-like-your-own AFS host parent, knew I should say something—explain that when we eat out as a family, we tend to avoid the more expensive dishes. That feeding a family with multiple kids gets pricey, and so we each do our part to remain cognizant of the cost. Instead, I just smiled.

To his credit, when the bill came, he offered to pay for his meal, outwardly acknowledging the price. I was relieved with his basic awareness but disappointed I didn't have the candor to express our budgetary constraints.

"Thank you for offering, but it's okay. We'll cover it. You're part of our family now."

Treat him like my own; the mantra pounded away in my conscience.

Okay, after this time.

11

"To Thine Own Self Be True...."

Depending on what reference source is used, this famous Shakespearean quote from *Hamlet* incorporates a variety of meanings. From a self-serving interpretation to doing the right thing, I found that our interactions and encounters with Rafael often straddled the various analyses of this quote, which, at times, conflicted with our natural inclinations. For each of us to continue to do, say, and believe what we previously did, and remain true to ourselves during the exchange seemed rather contradictory. If one of the main ideas behind an exchange involves opening one's eyes to a new way of things and appreciating differences, then staying true to thine own self poses a challenge in attempting to blend different cultures. "Staying true" to oneself revealed itself on many occasions with Rafael, disguised in different forms, some transparent and obvious, others more deep-rooted and engrained. At least initially, I believe Rafael's "self-benefitting" angle was not from conscious selfishness, but a result of limited life experiences and influences. Rafael was a kid, and he did what kids do in Freudian fashion, vacillating between his id and ego.

On one of the last few nights of summer, soon after Rafael's arrival, our family set out on a walk around the neighborhood loop. With the sun setting and the canopy of trees lining both sides of the street, the six of us conversed along the way, still in the honeymoon phase of getting to know one another. Crickets chirped, leaves rustled in the slight breeze, an occasional dog barked in the distance, and bats unthreateningly flew overhead. After a short distance, Rafael suddenly jumped into a squat position—body angled, feet spread, knees bent, and two fists clenched—braced for an attack. I, who frightens easily, recoiled. Frank and the kids stared at him.

"What are you doing?" they inquired.

"I heard something."

"What kind of something?"

"I'm not sure. But I'm ready," Rafael proudly declared.

"Ready for what?"

"If someone attacks me."

In that moment, we began to see a glimmer of Rafael's fight-or-flight response, a keen awareness honed from living in Brazil and Paraguay. It was a revelation to all of us, reminding us of the stark contrast in our environments. *How scary,* I thought, *to go about your life having to be so cautious.*

This was Rafael's truth.

Throughout my young adult life, the concept of volunteerism acquired a new meaning. After my undergraduate years as a biology major, being accepted into a master's program for physical therapy became my goal. All of the schools required volunteer work in order to gain exposure to the field. Upon completion of those requisite hours and the attainment of my degree, it wasn't until my forties that volunteer work began to take on more significance. Perhaps it was the fact that Alex would eventually be applying for college himself and I recognized the "game" that needed to be played to be accepted into a competitive school. College candidates wanted to appear humanitarian-minded. Despite this immediate ulterior motive, I strongly encouraged their volunteerism when possible to think outside of themselves. I hoped to cultivate in them a giving mindset and way of life.

During the first few months of our exchange, when opportunities arose requiring volunteers, I readily signed my kids up to participate. I included Rafael, whether it be serving food in our church, boxing meals for families in need, or cleaning up marshy wetlands in a neighboring coastal town. Sometimes these opportunities dictated an early morning rise. It was something I deliberately chose to discourage Rafael from sleeping until the afternoon on a weekend. I could sense he was not excited about this part of our lives, but he would oblige. Still, volunteerism was not natural for him, and he discredited it as "a waste of time."

On one particular day, we sat in church at tables arranged in a makeshift classroom setting, as construction to build a new parish center was underway. Arriving a few minutes early for our religious education class, we anticipated our chance to fall in line before the crowd, for the pre-class meal served cafeteria-style. Father Jack, our priest, called out to the parishioners, requesting the assistance of students to help serve the meals. To receive the Sacrament of Confirmation, students are expected to complete a minimum number of service hours, both within the church and the community. Zach, being in eighth grade, was one of the candidates, so serving meals would be an easy task to help meet his requirement. More importantly, though, I'd hoped opportunities such as these reiterated my credo: *Think of others. Be helpful. Be aware—aware of situations where you can help without being asked.*

Zach stood up and weaved between the tables and chairs. Almost naturally, Alex followed him, despite having already received his Confirmation. Emma, in sixth grade, was not yet a candidate and could have easily blended into the pool of non-participants—if I would have let her, which I did not. Making eye contact and with a slight tilt of my head, I gestured for her to follow her brothers.

I became engaged in light conversation with a friend several tables away, but after a few minutes, I realized Rafael remained seated at our table. Waving Emma over, I instructed her to encourage Rafael to assist with serving the parishioners.

Upon her return, she explained. "He doesn't want to. He said he doesn't have to. He thinks there's no point since he doesn't need service hours."

"Really?" I said.

"Yup."

Trying to mask my real feelings, a skill that frequently escapes me, I approached Rafael. "Hey, Rafael, why don't you go with Emma and help serve the food? Alex and Zach are over there, too."

"No, it's okay. I don't have to. I don't need to volunteer."

"Well, you're right. You don't have to. But that's the point of volunteer work. You don't have to. You don't do it for any reason other than to help because it's good to help others. So, go." My head tipped toward the food lines. "It's not a choice. It's what we do. My kids help."

Begrudgingly, he acquiesced.

At the time, I considered him selfish. Now, I recognize that his culture historically embraced the "take care of my own" mentality, where care extended only to friends and family, and this norm was all that Rafael knew. Only in recent years has serving others become a more widely-adopted concept in parts of South America. If only I had known this truth, then his tendency for inaction would have been vindicated, and my bitterness redefined.

I can look back now, to the night of the walk, when he got ready to fight what was probably a squirrel or stray cat. His fight-or-flight instincts were incredibly automatic. This was his South American upbringing, to be prepared for the dangers around you for survival sake; he was programmed for self-preservation, as well as self-mindedness. My children were raised in a very different type of community. Our family's experiences were different than anything he had seen before. I was just starting to comprehend that remaining "true to thine own self" was going to pose challenges for all of us.

12 Petunia

With the AFS family handbook as our bible, Frank and I introduced Rafael to our way of life. Logistical details were easy: *This is your bedroom, this is where the dirty laundry goes, this is the food pantry, make yourself at home.* Other aspects of the exchange year, however, were difficult to fully grasp. Independence from family, financial matters, and lifestyle inclinations were all concepts for which AFS had guidelines, though much was left to our comfort level and discretion.

It is a strange chemistry between host parents and exchange student, at least at the outset. I assume most experiences start out the same: everyone's innate craving to be liked and accepted is the driving force behind words and actions. However, once the honeymoon phase passes, first impressions wear off on both sides, and normal patterns of behavior and attitude become evident.

No matter how I tried, discussions with Rafael were different than with my own children. Alex, Zach, and Emma are rooted in the knowledge that, above all, we will always be family. That said, trying to convince all-knowing teenagers that we, the parents, are here to guide and educate can be exhausting. Enter an exchange student who has lived an entirely different life with varying values and priorities, then couple that with a natural and expected guard up toward strangers—not to mention the culture shock—and you can imagine how disconnected these talks felt.

During many of our teaching moments, although he politely obliged by listening, I wasn't certain how much my words actually resonated. After all, he was only going to be with us for a finite period. Maybe what he wanted out of his exchange was more simplistic—improve his English and have a great adventure in America. I aspired for a richer, deeper experience, one that would run its threads through the fabric of our futures. To accomplish that, I wanted our exchange experience to offer more than just a physical address that Rafael claimed during his stay. I wanted our home—our family—to represent significant life experiences and lessons that further contributed to his development into a respectable young man. For these reasons, I made it my duty to be a parent, not a hostess.

Soon after Rafael's arrival, it became clear that his full immersion into our home would have its obstacles. Whether it was a lack of understanding or compliance with AFS guidelines, we found ourselves engaged in a figurative tug-of-war, our family on one side, Rafael and his on the other.

Generally speaking, I am a rule-follower. Rules provide a framework, clarity, for order. One of the AFS guidelines involves communication between the exchange student and their natural family. Though AFS cannot prohibit contact between them, they do have suggestions to minimize adaptation difficulties. For me, these guidelines served as rules. I trusted what AFS claimed, that their suggestions were in place to help students achieve immersion quickly and in the best way possible.

"Homesickness can become a common problem for participants if they, and/or their families and friends, call frequently. During 'voice-to-voice' interaction, participants are reminded of their home culture, language, customs, and home activities at a time when they are feeling especially vulnerable in an unfamiliar environment. The sound of a loved one's voice can cause sadness for hours or days, as participants are constantly reminded of the distance and the differences around them. This sadness adds to the difficulties of adaptation, as participants are distracted from integrating into their host community. It is ideal to keep in touch primarily through email and to make calls only on special occasions, such as birthdays and holidays. We recommend that students connect with their families no more than once a week via email and that they have 'voice-to-voice' communication no more than once a month for about a half hour per call."

Multiple factors complicated these communication guidelines. First, Rafael was a fifteen-year-old adolescent, close to his family, for whom there was a possible communication barrier, resulting in lack of understanding of the immersion process. Second, in our technologically-driven society, the desire for instant gratification—encouraged by cell phone convenience—undermined the rules set in place. In other words, these handbook guidelines were authored prior to texting. In our early observations of Rafael, his frequent texts or Skype sessions were always in excess of the recommended amount, both in frequency and duration. Almost routinely, Frank or I tapped an index finger on the top of our wrist for him to bring closure to his correspondence.

In empathizing with this parent/child separation, I encouraged Rafael to send his family weekly emails as suggested. Hesitantly, he obliged one day, sitting at our kitchen table in his self-designated work space. He stared at his blank computer screen.

"I don't know what to write. What should I say?"

Feeding him topics that I thought would be of interest, I watched as he painstakingly drafted the first and only email to his family.

As the months proceeded, any AFS-proposed communication went out the window as weekly Skype sessions took over. It seems so petty and dictatorial, the idea of limiting communication. But, in my mind, we were laying the groundwork, the structure for what was to come. Maybe I subconsciously knew we needed an understanding in our household. Without it, there was no hierarchy between parent and child, no credence in our host-parenting approach. It was the apparent indifference to the AFS guidelines and the self-appointed exemption from them (by both Rafael and his family) that unnerved me. Why couldn't they just play by the rules? Were they finding the guidelines unbearable and missing one another more than expected? Or, perhaps they interpreted things differently and without a full understanding of how to facilitate Rafael's immersion? I wanted to be supportive during his transition yet simultaneously uphold AFS's suggestions for achieving maximum growth and enjoyment for each of us.

"Whatever my parents want, they get. They have a way," he volunteered one day. To hear Rafael make this claim rattled me.

It appeared we were housing a privileged foreign exchange student. Seeds of resentment would soon take root in the form of a metaphorical petunia, symbolizing anger and bitterness, a genus that originated in South America.

13

In Body, Not Mind

In South America, physical safety is a valid concern. The barbed wire and concrete fencing surrounding Rafael's home in Paraguay served as a testament to the measures necessary for his family's well-being. With both parents working, Rafael and Giovanna were latchkey kids. They were essentially housebound when not in school and, with limited adult guidance, technology became their go-to diversion. That fact was a reminder of how fortunate I was to be a stay-at-home mother.

Transitioning Rafael into our home exposed this great divide between his previous life and what we considered healthiest to facilitate a successful immersion. Excessive correspondence with his family and friends, combined with a habitual retreat into his technological world, set the tone. He was breaking rules left and right. Watching Portuguese movies, reading Portuguese news, frequently speaking in Portuguese with another Brazilian exchange student. All no-no's, according to AFS. He didn't express homesickness, but any outward signs of growth seemed stunted compared to other exchange students. Nothing earth-shattering, but still rattling to control-freak me. What troubled me was the implication that Rafael was with us in body, but not in mind. The fact that he held onto various comforts of his South American life, though natural, hindered his ability to fully embrace his exchange. I felt like he was trapped in a revolving door, circling around and around, stuck somewhere between in and out.

Almost immediately into his stay, Rafael began announcing a future date, November twenty-first. Imprinted in his mind, the date signified a hallmark moment in the months to come. Like his birthday, like a savior, or possibly the pinnacle of his exchange year, he eagerly awaited the day that PlayStation would release their new console. Unusual for a teenager? Not at all. However, staying up late on a weekend playing video games and then sleeping through half of the next day was not part of our family's routine. Despite it being acceptable within his own home, and many others, it was not something I supported. There were so many experiences to be had, especially during an exchange year in a different country. Sleeping away valuable daylight time negated Rafael's physical "availability" to living as a true member of our family.

One day in the car, Rafael peered out the window of his rear seat.

"How far is Walmart?" he inquired.

"About fifteen minutes. Why do you ask?"

"If you are able to, can you drive me there on November twenty-first, so I can buy the new PlayStation? If you can't, how much do you think a taxi will cost?"

I was stunned. I could not believe the urgency and priority given to video games. Though I recognize the countless people who anticipated the same "event," it still boggled my mind. Just hearing the types of games he enjoyed rubbed me the wrong way. *Call of Duty*, *Assassin's Creed*, and *Grand Theft Auto* were his favorites. Due to the explicit, mature, and violent material, all of them had earned a banned status from our home even prior to his arrival.

"We'll see," I told Rafael, not committing one way or another.

What he didn't realize, and what I consciously refrained from telling him, was that unless you stand in line all night long or pre-order a wildly popular item like a new video game or Apple gadget, chances of walking in on release day and purchasing them were slim.

Our immediate goal of getting him to disconnect with anything or anyone reminiscent of home, including his native language, continued to test us. I felt like a broken record spinning endlessly, churning out the same grating tune.

One day, I finally asked Rafael, "Why are you here? Why did you want to participate in an exchange program?"

"To have a good time," he replied.

I about lost it.

"This is not a vacation. I did not agree to do this for entertainment's sake. This was supposed to be an educational experience. You supposedly wanted to improve your English," I ticked off my mental list. Are you kidding me? This kid wanted a good time. Wrong answer.

14

What Is Time?

Ah, time. The barometer that measures life's passing moments that can never be relived. From the start of parenting, my daily approach toward child-rearing has been to fill it. Fill up the time. As a stay-at-home mother, strategizing about various ways to keep my young children active and stimulated brought structure to our days. Feeding time, playtime, naptime, repeat. Playtime in our house involved playdates, music and movement classes, open gym activities at various YMCA's, story hour at the library, and innumerable day trips to parks, playgrounds, zoos, aquariums, and children's museums. I became adept at scheduling the kids' and my days to retain sanity for all of us.

As the kids grew, afterschool activities soon crept into our schedules. We moved from East Providence to southern Rhode Island and, within a few years, Alex, Zach, and Emma were enrolled in almost everything that we viewed as beneficial. Their lessons and practices in soccer, dance, piano, karate, swimming, and skiing kept us constantly busy. Let it be noted, I do not complain about this period in our lives. Much of this was a luxury I chose and directed, and their activities served as investments for their futures, often yielding trophies, awards, and tangible measures of "success." The greatest significance of our busy lives was fostering a sense of commitment, confidence, work ethic, time management, and enjoyment in numerous developing skill sets for each of them. In addition, spending time *doing* things meant less time to be wasted. And less opportunity for our kids to get themselves into trouble.

In the summer of an upcoming school season, the high school fall sports teams hold captains' practices. Organized and run by selected leaders, these practices strive to condition the players to perform well at tryouts. When Rafael joined our household, Alex aspired to make the varsity soccer team. As a sophomore, the number of available spots for new players was hopeful, considering his skill level and work ethic. However, disregarding this, he anticipated what needed to be demonstrated to earn one of the coveted spots on the varsity team. When the first captains' practice was held that season, we encouraged Rafael to participate, assuming he would be interested in playing for either the JV or varsity team. After all, he was a Brazilian with a penchant for soccer. He often played it at home or in video games, and he watched professional matches when able.

On one August night, while dropping Alex and Rafael off at the soccer field for the first practice, I wished them good luck. I wanted them to do well and enjoy it, hoping for an overall positive experience for both of them. After picking them up from practice later that evening, when Alex and I were alone, I had the opportunity to ask about practice.

"So how did it go? How did you feel about it?"

"It was okay. We did the usual stuff, running and drills, that kind of thing."

"Did you feel okay about everything, or was it hard?"

"Honestly, I am a little worried," Alex disclosed.

"What about?" I inquired.

"Well, when we had to run, we had to go around the field. I always try to stay at the front of the pack, but I noticed Rafael was falling behind. I felt bad for him, so I dropped back to run with him. I mean, I know it's only captains' practice, but I really want to do my best, so I can make the varsity team. If I run at the back of the group, the coaches might think I'm not good enough, or that I can't keep up. But I still feel bad for Rafael, so I don't know what I should do."

Alex was in a tough spot. I was proud of him for caring, but I also recognized his predicament. I wasn't sure how to advise him, so only words of reassurance were offered.

A couple of days later, Rafael unknowingly provided a solution to Alex's internal struggle.

"I don't think I'm going to captains' practice tonight."

"Oh? Why not?" I asked.

"I don't think I want to play at such an intense level. At home, I play more for fun. Here, things are more serious. I don't want that kind of commitment."

While the tiger mom in me would typically discourage noncommitment, in this instance, it would satisfy both Rafael's and Alex's wants. Still, because I strongly believed that Rafael needed structured time, we considered an alternative.

"How about recreational soccer? They only practice like one time a week, then one game on weekends. That way it will be more relaxed and less of a commitment, but you'll still get some exercise and meet people."

Rafael was on board with the idea, and I was grateful for his effort to meet me halfway.

Shortly after Rafael's arrival, he casually revealed his inability to ride a bike, something not uncommon in Brazil. Feeling this was an easily acquirable skill, Frank set out to teach Rafael one fall day. Equipping him with a helmet and preliminary instructions, Frank coached him as he sat on a bicycle, attempting to balance on two wheels.

"You can't really balance when you aren't moving. It's a lot easier once you get going. Let's move to the street, it's flatter up there," Frank suggested, relocating themselves from the slant of our driveway.

After he briefed Rafael with the basics, Rafael mastered riding a bike in no time at all. Neighbors driving by slowed down to watch, with an occasional thumbs-up. Soon after, Alex, Zach, and Emma strapped on their helmets and hopped on their bikes to catch up with Rafael. The four of them pedaled away, rounding the loop and out of sight. A satisfying moment to watch for sure, one memorialized in the picture collage on a tumbler, a Christmas gift we gave him to capture this time and many more.

Considering that a recreational fall soccer season extends only a few months, and biking was only a leisurely activity for Rafael, I brainstormed about other possibilities in which he could take part year-round. In Paraguay and Brazil, certain cultural constraints hindered his exposure and access to the various opportunities afforded in America. Whether it was due to a lack of transportation, minimal school-based activities, or less importance given to padding college applications, Rafael had no experience with our busy lifestyle. After discovering he was a fan of mixed martial arts, I suggested he take karate classes, hoping that any similarities to Brazilian jiu-jitsu would help entice him. One of our former karate instructors, Sensei Bobby, had recently established his own dojo in our town.

One of Rafael's strengths was his willingness to try things. Fortunately, karate classes were an easy sell, and before long, Rafael was in attendance, beginning his martial arts experience as a requisite white belt student. Aside from the obvious physical benefits, what was especially valuable in my eyes were the abstract fundamentals of discipline, focus, and determination. Some aspects of Rafael's classes challenged him physically and mentally. Other aspects came easily, sparring being one of them. Unlike myself, who dreaded the one-on-one aggressive nature, Rafael seemed to relish in that.

"You should have seen Rafael in karate," Frank reported after picking him up from class one evening. "It looked like he was beating the crap out of the other kid."

I cringed, remembering how unnatural those interactions felt to me, encouraged to deliver offensive blows all the while defending against an attacking classmate. Perhaps his testosterone, machismo personality, and native environment made him well-suited for that. Regardless of the source of his drive, Rafael willingly and eagerly welcomed his karate class nights.

"Rafael, what is the biggest difference between your life here in the US compared to your life back home?" I asked him during one of our drives to the dojo. After a pause, he offered a brief reflection.

"Time. Back home, time goes so slowly. Here, we are always doing something. School, homework, activities. Time goes by so quickly here."

"Is that a good thing?" I curiously wondered aloud.

"I think so. It's good to be doing things. It gets boring at home," he concluded as he swung the passenger car door open and jumped out. "Thank you for driving me. See you later."

"Okay, have a good class."

I breathed a sigh of relief. We were filling his time. And he liked it.

Just as a child who counts down until his birthday or until Christmas, Rafael anxiously awaited November twenty-first. It came. It went. Just like that. No fanfare, no glory, no acquisition of a new PlayStation. Rafael was unsuccessful in locating a new system after numerous phone calls to local stores per my suggestion.

"That's okay, I'll keep trying." Rafael's reaction was surprisingly subdued. Perhaps the concept of time, and the possibilities of it, were a new discovery for him.

In retrospect, from a chronological distance and more insightful perspective, I can now recognize the lifestyle differences this entire phase brought to light. More so initially, Rafael's frequently chosen position in the car as a backseat passenger relegated me or Frank to the role of his chauffeur. Now, I wonder if it actually reflected his discomfort and lack of familiarity with us, and the back-row seating arrangement provided a physical and psychological separation. Or perhaps it was Rafael's way of showing us deference as the parents in charge. To this day, I don't know the answer. And his propensity for video games and electronics? That was just Rafael behaving like a typical teenager. It was his natural respite, his virtual escape, his time to disengage, which everybody needs. Even his inquiry about a taxi, despite being unusual in our small town, was a common mode of transportation in Paraguay or Brazil.

For me, this process has been a cognitive continuum. I have gradually realized many initial misperceptions and triggered emotions that were skewed by my own ignorance. This awareness has been a valuable educational perk, a gift that time has revealed.

15

If You Want Something Done Right, Do It Yourself

Fall is one of my favorite seasons of the year. The temperatures are perfect, and the colorful trees in our area are a sight to behold. However, with the perks comes the tedious task of raking leaves—a task our kids are often called upon to assist. Similar to our summer lawn-care routine, raking leaves means all-hands-on-deck to help distribute the workload.

In both Brazil and Paraguay, Rafael had no exposure to this sort of work. So, one day, when all four kids were available, we introduced Rafael to the drudgery of raking leaves. Based on the amount of foliage that drops on our lawn during the season, Frank established a system of raking the leaves into multiple piles, then used the tractor or wheelbarrow to move said piles beyond a rock wall on our property. As most people know, raking is not difficult, just monotonous. With the combined efforts of multiple people, however, it can be an organized and speedy task. Handing each of the kids a rake, Frank explained what we needed to accomplish, mostly for Rafael's benefit. Each of them chose separate locations in the yard and went to work. Unfortunately, Rafael's "contribution" immediately presented as fruitless labor. With earbuds plugged in, he spent the bulk of his time searching for good music on his phone. Comical at best, Frank redirected Rafael in his efforts, re-emphasizing how to maximize our effectiveness and efficiency.

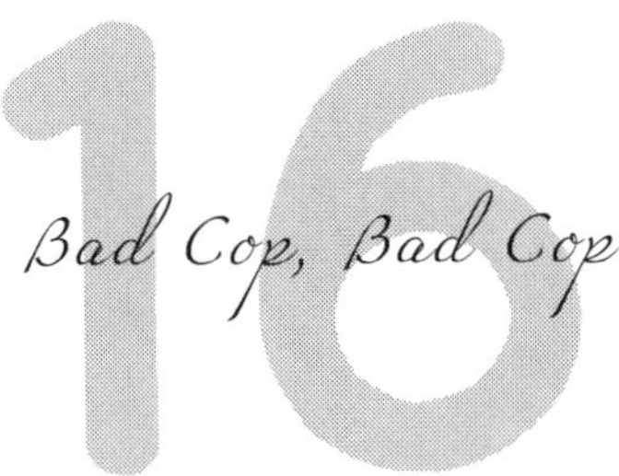

16 Bad Cop, Bad Cop

With the strides Rafael was achieving, we were discouraged when he announced his parents wanted to visit him in December. What? No other exchange student in our neighborhood or town spoke of a family visit, nor was it supposedly allowed by AFS, not this early into the program. If a natural family desired to schedule a visit, strict rules placed limitations as to when and under what conditions this should occur. Simply, scheduling a visit four months into Rafael's exchange violated the program's structure and undermined an authentic growth that was just beginning during our time together.

After he mentioned his family's intentions, and after our continued reminders to minimize anything impeding his immersion, my frustration level reached a limit. Other exchange students were approaching me at various functions and expressing unsolicited opinions about Rafael not adapting, not making friends, and reporting that his English-speaking capabilities were not progressing. When I checked Rafael's grades in school and realized he was failing two classes, it reinforced the uncertainty as to why Rafael agreed to do an exchange program. When something as trivial as choosing a pair of shoes prompted him to text his mother for approval, it gave me pause. Here he was, seemingly not becoming independent and not doing well on a variety of levels. The mere suggestion of his family's visit around the holidays sent me over the edge.

"We need to talk." The words spilled out of my mouth immediately after identifying myself to Linda, our regional AFS contact person. I explained our concerns suggesting Rafael's questionable acclimatization, then I capped off the diatribe with the mention of his family's planned visit in December.

"Really? That's not allowed."

"Someone needs to tell them that then," I explained.

"Okay, I will communicate with AFS Paraguay and ask them to speak with Rafael's parents and explain it to them," Linda offered.

"You know, Rafael mentioned his parents have a way of getting what they want."

"Ugh. All right, let me talk to some people and get back to you."

After various correspondences between me, AFS personnel, Rafael, and his mother, Leslie, a meeting was scheduled at our home. Leslie was aware that their desired visit was to be a topic of discussion.

Linda, Sonia (a designated local AFS liaison who served as a neutral party between the exchange student and host family), Rafael, and I sat around our dining room table. Rafael was braced for an ambush. Taking inventory of the adults in the room, he probably assumed no good cop was present to be his ally.

"Rafael, we have some concerns about your exchange," Linda initiated. "The Overlys say that there has been a lot of communication between you and your family, and they aren't sure if you are adjusting as well as you could be." She disclosed her knowledge of his excessive electronic use and lack of improvement in English in addition to other observations. She then reiterated the goals of an exchange program.

Rafael sat in silence.

"Furthermore, AFS does not allow for a natural family to come for a visit after only four months of a one-year program. It's not in your best interest or theirs. It will interfere with what we are all trying to achieve with this kind of experience."

Still, no response from Rafael.

With his family's December visit thwarted, our other main concerns—excessive correspondence and technology use—were addressed. Factors that prevented full immersion were discouraged. It was a one-sided conversation; Rafael respectfully silent. Eventually, we came to some sort of closing with my takeaway duty: a weaning Skype schedule, one that was predetermined, collaboratively agreed upon, and AFS-approved. Though not as stringent as that outlined in the family handbook, it was a fair compromise.

"Well, maybe they'll come after December," Rafael asserted.

Do petunias have thorns?

Swiper-Free

Q: What is required of an AFS Host Family?

A: As a host family, you will provide your student with:

1) *The opportunity to participate in your family's daily lives and events*
2) *The same care, support, and comfort you would another member of your family*
3) *A bed, not convertible or inflatable in nature; sharing a room with a sibling of the same gender close in age is fine*
4) *Three quality meals, including lunches and meals eaten as a family in restaurants*

Q: What is a host family's financial obligation:

A: AFS students arrive with their own spending money for social and school activities, clothes, etc. As a host family, you will not need to provide spending money or an allowance.

Q: Are host families paid?

A: No, host families are not paid. However, you will be entitled to a tax deduction each month that an AFS student stays in your home.

Once in a while in our community, teammates and their families go out to a restaurant after a soccer game. It serves as a bonding experience, encouraging cohesiveness on and off the field. After one of Alex's games, I sat across from another mother, Mary, at Applebee's. Ironically, she and her family were also hosting an exchange student, agreeing to the opportunity after hearing about our undertaking. As we reviewed the menu selections, I mentioned the "2 For $20" option to my kids and Rafael, implying that two entrées plus an appetizer for that price was inarguably the way to go. After several minutes of consideration, I asked what each of them planned to order. Alex, Zach, and Emma each chose an entrée from one of the various "2 For $20" items. When it was Rafael's turn to speak, he announced his selection, a burger similarly priced to our dishes, though not on the "2 For $20" list.

"Why are you letting him order what he wants? Why don't you tell him he has to order something from the '2 for $20' menu?" Mary opined.

"It's okay. His entrée is about ten bucks. That's pretty much the same price as ours, just without an appetizer," I rationalized. "At least it's not the shrimp."

"You have to tell him from the start, 'This is the way we do things in our family.' If you let him order whatever he wants from the beginning, he's going to keep doing that. Remember, we're supposed to treat them like our own kid. And if I tell my kids 'Pick something from this menu,' then that's what I'll tell my student, too."

I envied Mary's bluntness in establishing that understanding with her student. Perhaps she could anticipate the challenges ahead that I was unable to predict. Regardless, I stayed the course. Avoiding any awkward discussion with Rafael regarding money matters, I listened as "my" four kids ordered their respective meals, Rafael's burger included. And I smiled. Again.

Next time….

Countless financial situations with Rafael arose during his stay. And, to be perfectly clear, it was never about him or his family trying to take advantage of us. In fact, covering his fair share was not the problem. His family was always generous, sending numerous gifts for all of us and encouraging Rafael to purchase birthday and Christmas presents for our entire family. His parents paid for his activities, clothes, school supplies, or other big-ticket items. They possessed financial means, and Rafael benefitted from the use of a credit card. It became a sticky undercurrent with our kids, that Rafael would use his "swiper-free" card to magically acquire purchases without assuming the debt incurred from that form of spending.

Gradually, Frank and I became more deliberate at insinuating financial guidelines when dining out with the family. As we were expected to pay for Rafael, I thought it was only fair to ask of him the same as our own children. In general, Rafael followed suit, choosing meals comparably priced to ours. On multiple occasions, however, if he desired a more expensive item, he proposed to pay the difference above what we would normally cover. This is where his financial freedom stuck a thorn in my side.

It is difficult to explain, the strange logistical arrangement of housing another child. You agree to absorb many of the costs associated with daily living so, considering meals alone, three meals a day for many months affects how much a budget can responsibly extend for necessary expenses and "extras"—dining out being one of those. So, although Rafael could afford to order more expensive meals, it became a matter of principle. Here we were, asking our kids to mind the cost of things so we could continue to do and buy certain things to which we were accustomed and enjoyed. Many times, each child was asked to pick a smaller size (ice cream cone), order water instead of soda, or realize that Christmas would be different this year. Now we had to divide the same financial pot over four kids instead of three. If we asked Alex, Zach, and Emma to make sacrifices during this exchange, then I felt it was only right and fair that the same be asked of Rafael. If not, how do you think our kids would feel ordering their small ice cream cone, only to have him order his large one? How did it feel to them, sharing everything that was theirs (including us, their parents), but without a sense of mutual sacrifice? So, although there was the part of me that could have just accepted his monetary capabilities, it was a tough pill to swallow when confronted with numerous reminders of just that. As if to say that what we offered wasn't enough. And that stung. Because all that we offered was everything we had.

I struggled with guilt and the constant inner battle of what to let go. I knew some of what I felt was natural, but I was also embarrassed to think that I was being petty. In speaking with other host families, however, I found that my ambivalence and early feelings of resentment were not unique to just our household. Other hosts faced students accustomed to frequent world travel, second homes, and high-end possessions that prompted seemingly insensitive and ungrateful remarks. Why we host families began this exchange experience without realizing that many of these students were affluent is a mystery. Maybe it's because we had some preconceived notion that our student would be less fortunate and express outward appreciation for all we provided them. So, although I shared similar, justified emotions to others, it didn't change the fact that I frequently had to digest this financial aspect as what it was, something not to be controlled or changed by me. That over time, I had to accept Rafael's swiper-free attitude as innocent and unaware. After all, he was just a kid without the benefit of adult life experiences. We were purely different people with different lives and with varying perspectives. Hence, the basis of an exchange.

18 Oh, Crap....

Like many families, when our kids were very young, they wanted a pet, namely a dog. Knowing full well that they had no idea what taking care of a dog actually meant, Frank and I appeased them with an offer of a guinea pig. Surely a smaller animal meant easier, right? Alex, Zach, and Emma were delighted, picking out the cage and accompanying accessories, agreeing on the name Cheerio. Regrettably, Cheerio lived an isolated and idle life. Our initial attempts at walking her on a leash (yes, can you picture it?) were short-lived, as a rodent has a mind of its own and she would have no part of it. Unfortunately, Cheerio succumbed to what we assume was a malignant mass, so after her demise, the notion of a family dog once again became a hot topic.

"You know a dog is a lot more responsibility than a guinea pig," I proffered.

"We know, we know. We'll walk it and feed it and everything else. We promise!"

Being a cat person my whole life but knowing that was not a viable consolation for allergy-prone Alex or Frank, I mentally conceded to the images of absorbing a dog and the added workload into our household. The kids were now a few years older and could assume more pet-care duties. Without telling the kids, Frank and I selected a local breeder, a contact provided to us by a friend, who was a proud, new owner of a Labradoodle puppy. Touted as non-shedding and hypo-allergenic, this crossbreed of Labrador Retriever and Poodle enticed us. During several secret meetings with the breeder, I was afforded the opportunity to observe her new litter of puppies and their evolving temperaments. I readily and unfailingly gravitated to the same one. Choosing him, I bombarded the breeder with questions. Finally, sensing the breeder's annoyance with me, I ended my barrage and arranged for a future date to return and surprise the kids with our new family addition.

We piled the kids into the car one sunny, summer August day.

"Dad has to go meet with someone from work, then we'll go grab dinner or do something afterward." The discontent on their faces was unmistakable.

"Why do we have to come then? Can't you just stay home with us?" they whined. Not accustomed to telling white lies, I had to think fast.

"Because I don't feel like staying home and it'll be quick."

Twenty minutes later, we arrived at the breeder's house. The metal fencing surrounding the property served as a necessity as countless dogs greeted our car on the gravel driveway. I warned the kids not to get too close to the fence. Alex, Zach, and Emma adhered to museum rules: look, but don't touch. The barking worked as an effective deterrent, discouraging any of them from poking a single finger through the fence. The breeder suddenly appeared, reassuring that the dogs were curious but not dangerous.

Unlocking the gate, she escorted us through the pack of dogs, all encircling us to discover what wondrous new scents we brought from the outside world. Emma cowered behind our legs, shuffling along as we walked, maintaining coverage at all times.

Once upstairs in the breeder's home, the sight of a blue plastic kiddie pool in the middle of the floor caught us by surprise. Approximately eight puppies, in varying shades of apricot to reddish-hued, clumsily maneuvered their developing bodies around and on top of one another. The sloping sides of the pool proved to hinder their attempts at nimbleness.

"Aww, they're so cute," Emma purred, her previous distress forgotten.

"They are awfully cute. Do you guys want one?"

All three kids were momentarily speechless.

"What do you mean? Like, we're getting a dog?"

Divulging my prior secret visits to the breeder, we explained that, yes, I (the sole holdout in our family) was finally amenable to joining the world of dog owners.

"Remember, you all promised you would help take care of him. Not just the easy and fun stuff. A dog means responsibility, you know that?" I reiterated.

"We know, we know!" the kids vehemently affirmed.

Several years prior to Rafael's arrival, Alex, Zach, and I received our black belts in karate. Years of commitment, discipline, and determination are now reflected in the conglomeration of nunchucks, bo staffs, and kamas displayed on our basement wall. Albeit painstaking at times, our innumerable hours of karate classes culminated in the attainment of our black belts, a proud closure to that chapter in our lives.

As many parents know, if you ask a question, you will often get as many different responses as there are kids. Simply choosing a restaurant, Netflix movie, or pizza topping can become a laborious task when trying to satisfy different wants. Taking this into consideration, Frank and I thought it best to pre-select a dog name and present it as a suggestion to the kids, up for reasonable debate. We proposed the name Ike, short for Aikido, a Japanese martial art loosely signifying our karate background. Frank liked the simple but strong name, and I became attached to the Zen-like sentiment behind it. Plainly translated, Aikido means harmony. Soon after conferring with the kids, they, too, embraced the name and professed their acceptance of the new obligations that Ike would bring.

Despite the typical house-training issues, after months of bonding through the struggles and cuddles, Ike became our much-loved family dog. He was like a small stuffed animal, a miniature version, predicted to grow to only 20-25 pounds. But he was better than a toy; he was warm, soft, playful and alive. It surprised me how much I cherished his presence, and I couldn't imagine not having him as part of the Overly family. When I first saw pictures of Rafael holding his dog, I assumed that he felt the same way about pets and would adopt our love for Ike. Fairly transparent from the start though, Rafael's demeanor toward Ike was telling: at best, he ignored him. Though Rafael denied any fear of Ike, his body language, especially when riding in the car, was puzzling. If Ike sat next to Rafael, both of Rafael's hands grasped one of the interior side-ceiling grab handles as if preparing for a car accident. Eventually, we came to terms with Rafael not loving our dog.

In many households, regardless of culture, the delegation of age-appropriate chores to each family member exists. Ours is no different, and Frank and I value the developing responsibility encouraged by such a division of labor. From the beginning of Ike's introduction into our home, feeding and walking him was the minimal contribution expected of Alex, Zach, and Emma. Walking him included collecting his feces, especially when deposited off our property. For the sake of our neighbors, we required that our kids comply with this cardinal rule. We mistakenly assumed Rafael abided by the same requirement for his dog, Floppy.

While driving home one day after countless errands, my phone rang.

"Mom, we're having an issue." Alex's whisper was barely audible.

"What kind of issue? Who's having an issue?"

"Rafael and I took Ike for a walk. Ike pooped when we were going around the loop, so I asked him to pick it up. He won't. He's refusing, says it's gross."

"Do you have a bag?" I asked.

"Yeah, but he still won't," Alex frustratingly relayed.

"So, what are you doing?"

"We're staring at it. The pile of poop."

I envisioned two teenage boys, standing only feet apart, towering over a brown lump on the ground, in a shit showdown.

"I explained to him that when we walk Ike, part of walking him means picking up his poop. That it's what we do."

"And?"

"That in our family, we each do our part, and that you and Dad do a lot of things for us, and that one of our jobs as the kids in this family is taking care of Ike, and that includes picking up his poop," Alex ranted in one long run-on sentence.

"And?"

"He said he was fine walking him, but he didn't expect to pick up the poop." Apparently, on any previous walks, Rafael had been spared this task. Now, it seemed fair was fair. Alex was ready to indoctrinate Rafael as the fourth Overly dog-owning child.

"So, what are you doing now?"

"Nothing. We're just standing here. We're around the loop, in front of one of the neighbor's houses."

"Okay, so try to explain to him again it's really not a choice, that we expect it of him. If that doesn't work, just stay where you are, and I'll come find you, and I'll talk to him. I'll be coming into the neighborhood in a few minutes." I was exasperated. This was our first experience with Rafael being blatantly defiant.

A few minutes later, my phone rang again.

"So, we're home now. After standing there for like ten minutes staring at the poop, he finally gave in. I told him, 'Rafael, my parents are doing a lot for you, too, you know. They're treating you like their own kid, all the good things, but that means you should also be responsible for the things that Zach, Emma, and I do, too. This is what we do in our family, in our world.'" Alex, always keeping the peace in a wise-beyond-his-years-way, had surprisingly stood his ground, literally and figuratively.

"Finally, he picked it up, but I can tell he's mad."

"Why do you say that?"

"Because now he won't speak to me. When we got home, he went inside the house, straight out the back door to the deck, and he's just standing there, staring into the woods."

Ugh, I thought. Why does something so small have to be a big deal?

After I got home, Rafael was quiet, more than usual. I asked if I could speak to him and we retreated to our upstairs bonus room, a centralized family room on the second floor. Providing privacy and neutrality, the bonus room was an impartial forum, equipped to handle lengthy conversations if necessary. Since Rafael's arrival, I hoped the bonus room symbolized a safe place to manage conflict and find resolution.

"So, do you want to tell me what happened? Why are you mad?" I inquired.

"I expected to walk the dog. I did not expect to pick up his poop."

"Well, you have a dog. Floppy. What do you do when Floppy goes to the bathroom?"

"She goes in the backyard."

"And?"

"Well, sometimes I…" Rafael concluded his sentence with his index and middle fingers pinched tightly to his thumb, with a crinkled nose and furrowed brow.

"Why sometimes?" I asked. "Why not all of the time?"

Rafael shrugged.

"I'll be honest. I know it's gross, but it has to be done. It's not a choice. We can't leave Ike's poop anywhere in the neighborhood. Other people, other animals, can step in it. It's not nice to look at.

So even if we can get away with not picking it up, that's not an option, so we expect it of our kids." Rafael remained silent. I wondered if somewhere in his mind, what had just transpired negated his fantasy of living the dream. The American dream. In this American world, dog poop and all.

19

Did He Really Just Say That?

Another reason I welcome fall is Thanksgiving. As we did not have family who lived near us during our early family-rearing years in Providence, Frank and I established our own holiday routines when Alex was two years old and Zach was just six months. One day, Frank attended a mandatory work seminar during which he met a young father named Chris. After briefly striking up a conversation, both men exchanged telephone numbers.

"I met someone at work. His name is Chris. He and his family just moved from Texas. Nice guy. His wife stays home too, and they have a little boy Alex's age. And they're pregnant with their second. Maybe you want to give her a call and you two could hang out," Frank suggested, fully aware of my craving for adult companionship during the long days of caring for a toddler and a baby. I hadn't met any friends in the area yet, and so the prospect excited me.

A few days later, I allowed my desperation for friendship to fuel a phone call.

"Hi, Diane? My name is Hannah, and our husbands met at work."

"Oh, hi. Chris told me you have a two-year-old son too?"

That's how our friendship began. Over the past sixteen years, our two families have experienced the highs and lows that life offers. We have celebrated many holidays and special occasions together as a surrogate family to each other, and our traditions have culminated in some of our most cherished memories. Though both of our families have moved, to a Boston suburb for them and southern Rhode Island for us, our regular get-togethers solidify the strong ties we've built. Thanksgiving continues to be one of our shared holidays, and it has been especially invaluable to our kids in light of the distance that contrasts with the frequent playdates we used to coordinate.

As our families grew, a total of seven children between us, Chris initiated a gratitude-inspired and required statement by the kids at Thanksgiving. First written and then read aloud, it was an abbreviated declaration of those things for which they were thankful. We as parents sat back to enjoy this exercise of calling to mind simple joys. The youngest child started first, lest he or she be intimidated by the more mature prose of an older sibling. Frank, Chris, Diane, and I applauded each of their efforts year after year. We appreciated the evolution in sentiment occurring and, more importantly, the kids' comfortable ability to sincerely reflect and express themselves.

Thanksgiving that year with Rafael was no different. Amidst the expected food gorging and the fathers vs. sons football game, Chris rallied the kids for that time set aside to compose their Thanksgiving "essays." Though none of our kids love the writing portion of this task, they do excitedly anticipate hearing what the others have to say. *Family. Friends. The tradition of our families being together.* These are the recurring concepts, year after year. Redundant, but heartfelt.

We explained to Rafael the purpose of this activity and we lowered our expectations of what he might produce considering the unfamiliarity of the task, not to mention English wasn't his first language. After each child hunkered down in separate areas of the house to create their written work, everyone reconvened in the family room to listen.

"I am thankful for my family," Nicholas shyly initiated.

"I am thankful for my friends," Sophia continued.

"I am thankful for all of this great food," one of the older children added.

Eventually, it was Rafael's turn. I'm not sure what I expected, but it surely wasn't what we heard.

"I am thankful for the air we breathe. And the food we eat. I am thankful for my PlayStation," he began, referring to his recent fluke in obtaining one. Somewhere in his speech, he made a brief and casual mention of us, his American family. "But what I am most thankful for is my family and country. Brazil is the best country in the whole world, and there's nowhere I'd rather be. It's the only place for me."

We were speechless. It felt like a slap in the face. I looked at Diane and she whispered out of the corner of her mouth.

"Did he really just say that? How does that make you feel?"

Simply hearing her questions validated my impulse emotion of feeling devalued. I certainly didn't want Rafael telling falsehoods, and I didn't expect him to profess anything extraordinary, at least not in relation to his exchange year, America, or us, for that matter. But I did not anticipate hearing words that were full of pride to Rafael but felt incredibly belittling to me. I wanted to believe it was just his age, that Rafael was incapable of filtering thoughts into politically-correct spoken ideas, in English anyway.

A couple of days later, I thought it was appropriate to speak with Rafael regarding his essay. I specifically remarked about his admirable and natural allegiance to Brazil, but that I perceived his "truths" as offensive. The most challenging aspect of this conversation, though, was conveying how his words were hurtful, despite lack of intention. I didn't want to come across as jealous or insecure. Instead, I instructed Rafael on how to sensitively craft his ideas, especially considering time, place, circumstance, and target audience. It was truly a lesson in diplomacy and tact, a skill he could develop and benefit from in all areas of life, from that day forward.

20 We Accept

Remember the issue of how long Rafael would be with our family? Upon our initial consent to serve as his host family, a semester had been our agreement. Within that time, we had the ability to assess the experience and extend his stay with us if we desired.

Sometime in the late fall or early winter, with the holidays approaching, I received a phone call from AFS, inquiring about our decision. Should he stay, or should he go? That was the question. During a rare opportunity with Frank, Alex, Zach, and Emma converged in our kitchen at the same time, I addressed the proverbial elephant in the room.

"So, what do you guys think? AFS wants to know if we want to keep Rafael for the year. If not, they have to start making plans to find him a new family in town."

"What do you want?" the four of them searched for my lead.

"I'm not sure. It hasn't been totally easy, you know," I said.

Alex, with almost a stream-of-consciousness rationale, came to Rafael's rescue. "I think it'd be weird…you know, sending him away to another family, another house in our town. He'd have to adjust again. It'd be like we're all still going to the same school and I'd pass him in the hallway with my friends. They'd say, 'Alex, there's your exchange student' and I would have to say, 'Not anymore. We kicked him out.' How mean would that be? Everyone would think we're jerks. No other host family in our town is only doing a semester. I think we should keep him."

What started out as one of our truths, that Rafael could move to another host family's home after one semester, did not play out as an option. Looking back, both Frank and I truly knew that a semester stay provided a comforting recourse if necessary, but realistically, we'd have Rafael for the year. We wanted it to work. We wanted it to be a great experience for all. How could we give up halfway through and not see it to the end? That kind of attitude went against everything I'd been teaching my kids. And although I developed a terrible case of acid reflux during the exchange, which I attributed to the associated logistics and stressors of having four kids, I approved the invitation to ask Rafael to stay with us. When I made the call to AFS to reveal our willingness, they were ecstatic. Not only would it save them time and resources locating a new host family, but perhaps it also painted the illusion that, thus far, our exchange experience was turning out to be a success. Though that would have been presumptuous, Frank and I were willing to heed Alex's concerns and commit to what we felt was right.

When we finally had the chance to sit down with Rafael for a few minutes, we delivered our proposal for him to continue the year with us. Funny, a thought suddenly washed over me that he could reject us. He could have said that he hated being with our family, in our home, and he wanted to try somewhere new. Fortunately for our egos, the idea proved to be a cursory thought as Rafael exhaled in relief.

"I was so worried, you know. When I came here, I wasn't sure what would happen to me if I had to change families and homes. Where I would go? So, this makes me very happy. I like being here with all of you," he disclosed. Vulnerability was not a trait we normally saw in Rafael. "My parents will be so happy, too. We kept wondering what was going to happen, so now we don't have to think about that anymore."

Despite our struggles as a host family, little and big, I realized I often forgot that Rafael was a fifteen-year-old child. A kid. No matter how self-sufficient and stoic he seemed on the outside, he still wanted to be accepted on the inside. My attempts at parenting him sometimes overshadowed those details. This was all new to him. This country, this family, this home and way of doing things. It was an epiphany. In essence, Rafael and his family were at our mercy. Their sense of security hinged on us wanting to keep him. After all, no one wants to feel rejected. Isn't that the truth? At that moment, I started to see more clearly.

21
Let It Snow!

As beautiful as a newly-fallen snow blanket lays on the ground, its associated hardships are just as evident. Travel becomes more challenging, layers of clothing need to be added, and night seems to fall faster. For Rafael, he could hardly wait to experience it for the first time. When the first flurries of the season began to float from the sky one winter morning, I texted him at school to tell him to look outside.

I know, I saw it already! he responded via a caption to a picture of him standing outside of the school. Though my first thought was, *What is he doing outside during school hours? I hope he doesn't get in trouble*, I was so happy for him.

Mother Nature dealt us a harsh winter that year. In the recent past, our area typically received only a couple of relatively big snowfalls, sufficient to either delay or cancel school. But during Rafael's exchange year, the snow seemed to never cease. We could barely clean off our sidewalks, driveways, and roads when another storm would dump yet another load onto the existing piles.

Most kids feel elated when they find out that school has been canceled due to snow. Donning snow clothes, building forts, and having snowball fights trump school any day. I know it. I was a kid once, and my kids are no different. To see Rafael's awe with snow, to witness his first times playing in it, remains a great memory. Seeing it through his eyes was surprisingly gratifying. As if I felt that, somehow, we provided him this incomparable life event, one he would attribute to being with us.

Though relaxing, the novelty of snow days eventually wears off for most students. Canceled school days equate to make-up days added to the end of the semester. For Rafael, this reality didn't minimize that he wanted every day to be a snow day. He often lamented that two-day weekends were insufficient, even though I did not perceive him to be overworked or overstressed from his American education. His lackluster grades and ample downtime reinforced he was not what I envisioned in an assumed high-achieving exchange student.

One winter evening, after a phone call announcing yet another school cancellation the following day due to an imminent storm, I heard celebration in the kitchen. Descending the stairs onto the first level of our house, I immediately understood. All four kids had heard the snow day message from the school district, and the noise I heard was that of Rafael. Naked from the waist up, he swung his shirt around his head while prancing around the kitchen island in Mardi Gras-like revelry.

Though I knew he was just being an ordinary kid, I wished for a glimpse of the disciplined standards I wanted to see. Were school and our way of life that taxing compared to Rafael's life back home? Snow or no snow, I just didn't want this exchange year to be Rafael's vacation. I wanted it to be life-changing.

22

If You Want Something Done Right...Part 2

Recall Rafael's attempts at raking leaves? Now, mentally exchange the rake for a shovel, a warm-hued nature scene for a snowy one devoid of color, and work gloves for winter gloves. That basically depicts our snow-shoveling lesson with Rafael. Enough said.

23

The Land of Opportunity

America the Beautiful. It is one of our patriotic taglines enticing immigrants and tourists to experience firsthand all our country has to offer. We tend to take for granted those things to which we are accustomed, including the liberties and cultural benefits. Often, it is only through another's eyes that we're reminded of the opportunities we have.

Going to New York City at Christmastime is a traditional holiday highlight for our family, as well as for the millions of visitors that stampede through the city. Seeing Broadway shows, shopping at Times Square, ice skating at Rockefeller Plaza,

and browsing Macy's front window displays are just some of the draws luring people to visit this concrete jungle. The kids and I love to soak it all in, whereas Frank experiences sensory overload. Hence, our annual mini-vacation to NYC usually spans only a couple of days and nights. Regardless of its short duration, the trip would give Rafael a taste of the Big Apple, and possibly even a familiar comfort, assuming any shared similarities with his former stomping ground, São Paulo, Brazil.

Our NYC trip proved to be as enjoyable as usual, marked by the stereotypical tourist traps like the Statue of Liberty and Chinatown. When it was time to return home, the kids settled into the car, their souvenirs safely tucked inside their backpacks. Our several-hour drive spanned over dinnertime and, aiming to drive sufficiently away from most city traffic, we chose a Connecticut rest area as our intended dining location. Once there, we filled our bellies quickly. Meals and bathroom breaks concluded, the kids hunkered down in their car seats, removing their shoes and coats for maximum comfort, popping in earbuds. Almost instantly, Rafael signaled something was amiss.

"Uh oh, I can't find my backpack."

"Is it under your feet?" I asked, eyeing the assortment of apparel and blankets heaped on the car floor.

Rummaging through everything, the kids concurred. "Nope. Not here."

"I must have left it at the rest area. It's gone, I'm sure. It had my laptop and everything. Someone probably found it by now and took it."

"I guess we'll turn around then and go back to the rest stop."

Frank drove to the next immediate exit on I-95 then detoured southward.

"I know it's gone. There's no way it's still there. Someone would have taken it," Rafael resigned.

Frank raced against time with the hope of retrieving Rafael's belongings. As soon as Frank parked the car, Rafael sprinted inside.

"I don't know. This might not be good. What are the chances it's still there?" we all questioned.

After several minutes, Rafael reappeared, breathing hard.

"I found it!" he exclaimed. "I went back to the spot we were sitting, but it wasn't there. So, I asked someone, and they had it behind the counter. Someone must have found it and turned it in." Rafael was awestruck. "I can't believe it. Back home, that would have been gone. Someone would have stolen it without a doubt. There's no way…."

Knowing what had been at stake, we all shared his relief. Not only that but, in my mind, I celebrated our land of opportunity. Not in the self-serving, opportunistic kind of way, but rather in a proud-to-be-an-American way. Yes, Rafael's backpack could have easily been stolen, but it wasn't in this case. It affirmed an opportunity of selfless kindness and empathy from an anonymous stranger. An opportunity for Rafael to mentally challenge what would have been a given in his natural environment. A seemingly small act, but one with a lasting impression.

24

Are We Having Fun Yet?

It's a curious wonder that many people love roller coasters. The way they make you feel dread and fun all at the same time. The way you think you know, but don't always, what comes after the next hill, dip, or turn. Even when your ride ends, sometimes you're not sure if you liked it or not. Maybe it's the unpredictability. Maybe it's the ups and downs, leaving your stomach questioning your participation. But something about it lures you back.

Similarly, I feel like our exchange year was a rollercoaster. It drained us yet invigorated us. It physically and psychologically jarred us as much as it thrilled with surprise. I never knew what to expect. I never knew what the next day would bring.

25 Risk vs. Reward

Skiing has been one of Frank's passions since his childhood. I, on the other hand, only learned to ski while dating him, my first experience in college. Year after year, I became moderately competent at the sport. After having children, Frank fantasized about our family being a "ski family." Though it never provided me the joy it did him, I willingly submitted to raising Alex, Zach, and Emma as skiers, recognizing the value in adopting a healthy, outdoor activity we could do together. I had no desire to be holed up in a boring lodge, waiting for hours, just to dispense lunch for a midday meal. Rather, I opted for inclusion in what could often be a cold, uncomfortable, and sometimes risky sport.

The kids' winter break typically fell in February. Many families booked tropical vacation getaways, while some complemented their winter season with an escape to a mountain resort for skiing or snowboarding. Our family was one of the latter. A visit to a

Vermont or New Hampshire mountain range became a traditional family trip, and we were eager to include Rafael.

Frank and I discussed how our annual ski vacation would play out, considering that Rafael had just experienced snow for the first time, and skiing was a far cry from snowball fights and snow angels.

"Obviously, Rafael would probably prefer to come with us," I predicted.

"But we have to remember that he doesn't know how to ski, so he won't want to sit in a lodge or hotel room all day by himself," Frank stated. "Even if he takes lessons and does okay, chances are he won't be able to ski with the boys and me." The implications of Rafael possibly skiing with Emma and me on the less advanced runs caused me no second thought, though I was uncertain how much fun it would be for him. Considering there were very few alternatives, we hatched a strategy.

"Well, Yawgoo is close by. Maybe we can propose that he take several lessons there, to prepare him for our trip in February—if his parents are agreeable," I suggested. "Then we'll see how he's doing when our trip comes around and figure it out from there."

Through the month of January and into February, Rafael registered to participate in four ski lessons at Yawgoo. Out of necessity, some of his lessons were scheduled in the evening based on school, wrestling practice, and homework. Though it was only a fifteen-minute drive from our home, with his lesson lasting a little over an hour, waiting for him inside the lodge made the most sense.

From the second-floor windows, I could observe his weekly progress.

Rafael's third lesson fell on a Saturday. Since neither Alex nor Zach had any prior commitments that day, I suggested they accompany us to Yawgoo. It would be a chance for them to put on their skis to warm up for our upcoming trip. Afterward, the three boys could ski together, and Alex and Zach could evaluate his ability level firsthand.

Recognizing the relative size of Yawgoo and its minimum number of available trails, I still simultaneously mentally acknowledged the possibility of physical injury while skiing. Considering that after Rafael's lesson ended, the three boys would be skiing sans any instructor, I remained inside the lodge just in case of emergency. I could have gone home, especially since I anticipated that several hours would elapse between the start of Rafael's lesson and the boys wrapping things up for the day. Had it just been Alex and Zach, I would have been comfortable leaving Yawgoo and returning later. However, keeping in mind Rafael's novice skier status, I thought it best to stay on site.

When Rafael concluded his lesson that day, he came into the lodge to rendezvous with Alex and Zach.

"Make sure you three stay together and don't go on any trails that are too hard for Rafael," I mandated. "Rafael, remember, being a good skier isn't about how fast you go. It's about how in control you are. Being able to turn and stop is what's important. You want to be safe at all times," I stated, envisioning accidental collisions with people and inanimate objects alike. "I'll be here in the lodge if you guys need anything."

Savoring my respite from driving duties, I strolled through the first floor of the lodge and people-watched, reveling in the fact that my boys were independent, and that I had some alone time.

Suddenly, without warning, frenetic voices whooshed into the lodge.

"Mom, Mom! Rafael's hurt!" It was Alex and Zach, barely recognizable to me under their face masks and headgear.

"What do you mean? Where is he?" My heart thumped nervously.

"He's coming in. But you should have seen him. We went down a black, and he did fine," the boys described, referencing the most advanced trail that Yawgoo offered. Had it been a different New England mountain resort, the steepness grade of a black diamond trail would have been more concerning. However, at Yawgoo, the classification of difficulty levels of their trails was skewed based on the lesser elevation the ski area possessed.

"We got to the part where the black trail levels off and merges with the green. We were ahead of him, so we stopped to wait, but he kept going right past us. We yelled, 'Rafael, stop!' He flew by us and said, 'Can't stop, gotta go!'"

I could only imagine the scene and shuddered in response.

"And?"

"It happened so fast. We thought he was heading toward the lodge and would wait for us at the bottom. But he kept picking up speed, and the point where he should have turned or stopped, he didn't. He started heading toward the area where the snow meets gravel. And there was a small building down there. Like where they store equipment and stuff," the boys continued. "When he got to that point, he skied right off the snow, over the gravel, and ran smack into the building. Then he crumpled. We thought he was dead. There was no movement for a while. We were so scared. We skied down there to check on him. He started to get up and it looked like he was okay." I could tell they were shaken by what had just transpired.

Oh my God. How on earth would I be able to tell Rafael's mother that he could have died or been injured? It brought back the dread I felt from years ago when I received a late-night phone call from my aunt telling me my father had been the victim of a random, violent mugging. His subsequent brain injury left him wheelchair-bound and cognitively and physically impaired for his remaining six years alive. I didn't even want to think about it.

"Where is he?!"

"Don't worry. We think he's okay, but he's coming in now."

Right then, as I looked past the boys in the direction of the swinging lodge doors, Rafael entered wearing a big, perplexing smile on his face. It was telling that he had no comprehension of the emotions we felt on his behalf, or of the very real chance of significant injuries with runaway skiing.

"Rafael, are you okay?"

"Yeah, but I think my knee is messed up," he indicated as he sat on a nearby bench.

"What do you mean?" I asked, attempting to get an inventory of any injuries.

"It hurts if I press on it here," Rafael specified, pointing to an area near his patella. I reached down to gently run my fingers over a goose egg that had formed.

"Other than that, does it hurt inside the joint? Does it feel like you can walk okay? Are there any other areas that hurt?" I asked.

Moving his other body parts, demonstrating to himself and me that everything worked, we unanimously agreed it was time to call it a day.

Wow, close call.

After icing his knee at home, I took the opportunity to speak with Rafael. His outward flippancy of the situation disturbed me. Was he covering up for any embarrassment he felt? Was I misinterpreting his stoicism as trivializing the seriousness of his accident?

"Rafael, I need to explain something to you," I began. "The boys are upset."

He looked puzzled.

"What you don't realize is that they were really afraid for you. They were scared. They thought you were badly hurt or dead," I explained. "I'm bothered, too. It seems like maybe you don't remember that we are responsible for your safety and, God forbid, if something happens to you, we would feel terrible. You know, they care about you, we all do. So please understand, don't take this situation lightly, and whatever you do, please don't make it seem like a joke because we're all still shaken up about it."

Rafael nodded.

A week after his skiing accident, Rafael attended his fourth and final lesson at Yawgoo. Using exercised caution, perhaps due to our talk, he concluded it with a seemingly newfound respect for the sport. Maybe in a counterintuitive way, Rafael's accident was a blessing in disguise, a reality check for him and us.

February break soon approached. With the SUV and Thule clamshell packed, little space remained for anything else outside of our six bodies, skis, poles, ski bags, food, and luggage.

Ironically, during our three-hour drive to the hotel, I received an email from Leslie, Rafael's mother. Having watched the Winter Olympics recently, she became overcome with concern about Rafael's safety. Knowing that he was participating in a sport in which she just witnessed professional skiers' lives in jeopardy, doing something in which they were ranked the best in the world, revved up her maternal instinct. I sent her a response trying to allay her fears, reiterating we would do everything in our power to keep Rafael safe.

"Rafael, your mom just sent me an email. She is really worried about you skiing. Did you tell her about your accident at Yawgoo?"

"No, she just worries."

"Well, I just told her that the skiing you would be doing isn't the same as what she saw the Olympic athletes doing." I knew in my heart that with skiing comes innate associated risks. So, although I was somewhat minimizing that fact to Leslie, the truth is that the same can be said about many activities in life. Hopefully, that's where good judgment helps.

"You need to be very careful. We don't want any of us getting hurt, but especially you. I feel more responsible for you than my own kids because your parents are trusting us. Please, please, please ski smart and ski safely." I was hoping Rafael's Yawgoo incident would be a guiding force, with God on our side, in making sound decisions on the slopes. I was also trusting in Frank to know how much was too much.

"You better keep him safe or they'll kill us," I half-jokingly said.

Over the span of three days, Frank and the boys got their money's worth by skiing long and aggressive days at various mountain resorts near our hotel. Typically, they chose trails more advanced than those Emma and I favored; thus, we would go on our separate way. Occasionally, however, all six of us convened to ski a few trails together as a family.

The weather was our friend that trip, emphasizing the beauty and serenity that skiing granted. On a glorious, sunny, and vista-rich day, I could truly appreciate and cherish those snapshot moments that drew people back to the mountains time and again. Rafael's skiing ability had eclipsed Emma's and mine in that short time and, truly, I was impressed with his sense of adventure, confidence, and aptitude.

Sitting shoulder-to-shoulder on a quad chairlift, we inhaled the crisp air as we skimmed the side edge of the snow-covered trees. Occasionally, a fleck of red or purple caught our eyes. For some strange reason related to an '80s form of rebellion, ladies' bras and beads were strewn on the branches. Seeing an unexpected pop of color exaggerated the backdrop of white.

"You're doing really well, Rafael," I complimented through my face mask.

"You think so? I hope so."

"Are you having fun?"

"Oh, I'm having so much fun!"

"Really?"

"Yes, this is awesome. It's so pretty here and so much fun," his voice trailed.

He dismounted the chairlift and followed Frank and the boys in pursuit, spraying me with a thin dusting of snow. During that sliver of passing time, I hoped it was an experience he'd never forget.

26 The Burden of Proof

Of the various activities Rafael took part in, wrestling was his chosen winter sport. As with all of the high school sports teams, an awards night is held honoring the athletes at the end of the season. MVP and sportsmanship awards are bestowed on deserving students, and those lettering also receive special recognition. In the least, each athlete receives a certificate for their contribution. In an attempt to distinguish the night, the majority of athletes arrive in semi-formal attire. Not all, but most.

Though some may not subscribe to the philosophy of "do as others do," in this case, I am a believer of an appropriate dress code. In general, when dressed up, people seem to carry themselves a certain way, behave accordingly, and convey a different sense of respectability. Obviously, it's up to each family to decide what attire is acceptable for what occasion. In our home, there are many a place and time for casual clothes—awards night is not one of them.

"So, Rafael, you have a sports awards night at the school tomorrow," I reminded him one winter day.

"What's that?"

"It's a special night when athletes receive recognition for participating in a school team. They hand out awards and certificates to everyone. You have to get dressed up."

"Dressed up? What do you mean?"

"Most guys wear a dress shirt and tie, some wear jackets. At least a nice shirt and tie," I specified.

"Really? That's dumb."

"No, it's not dumb. It's a way to make the night feel special, not just another school event where the kids wear athletic clothes. So, make sure you look nice."

Alex, present for this conversation, nodded in agreement.

The next morning, talk of the awards night that evening arose again.

"Rafael, remember to lay out a shirt if you need me to iron it for tonight. And don't forget a tie."

Rafael balked. "I don't think I need to wear one."

"You don't *need* to wear one but you're part of our family this year, you're an Overly, and I like the boys to wear a tie for special occasions. I think people view and treat you differently when you are dressed up."

"Rafael, you should wear a tie. Most guys do," Alex reiterated in support.

Later that day, neither Frank nor I were available to drive Rafael to the awards ceremony, so arrangements were made to have a neighbor kindly drive him to and from the school. Not long after we returned home, my husband and I were standing outside contemplating potential outdoor home improvements when our neighbor's car pulled in our driveway sooner than expected. Rafael climbed out and bounded down the asphalt. With what seemed to be a skip in his step, he announced, "The ceremony was quick. For some reason, the coach wasn't even there."

I could barely process his words, which were overshadowed by the glaring absence of a tie.

"Rafael, where is your tie?" I seethed.

Rafael held a finger to his lips and paused with a smirk.

"I forgot it."

Following him into the house, I tried my hardest to keep my emotions at bay. "Rafael, sit. We need to talk."

He looked at me quizzically.

"I have a really hard time believing you forgot to wear a tie. We had a long conversation about it yesterday and this morning and Alex even told you that you should wear one."

"Well, when I was getting dressed, I just forgot."

"So, you mean to tell me that in putting on your nice pants and shirt, you happened to forget a tie, even though we made a big deal about it."

"Yes."

"Well, I don't believe you. And that's a really bad feeling."

"Well, you can't prove I didn't forget."

"You're right. But you can't prove you did."

Stalemate.

27

Boston Cream, Anyone?

Black and white. That's how I described Rafael, a concept with which he actually agreed. It's fitting that his favorite donut was Boston cream, a combination of a rich, dark chocolate frosting in contrast with the vanilla custard injected in the center. He was a person of such extremes, not unlike me, but different. Where Rafael was often black and white when it came to the quantity of things, I am black and white (i.e., rigid) in principles. Regardless of each of our different tendencies, and because of our strong and sometimes inflexible personalities, I attempt to find balance related to most things in my days and I tried to persuade Rafael to do the same. To discover moderation, to find the "gray."

Rafael is stubborn. A personality strength or flaw, depending on how you look at it. Unfortunately, in some of our interactions, that stubbornness played out in a negative manner. It was a current against which we swam. It was a truth that, at times, interfered with the objectives of his exchange.

Dissimilar to our boys, Rafael had a hearty appetite. He seemed to relish tasty delights such as hamburgers, donuts, Pop-Tarts, Reese's Peanut Butter Cups, and ice cream. Granted, part of the appeal was in the novelty. Especially enticing though was the fact that swiper-free spending garnered an unending supply. However, after months of Rafael gaining weight (25 pounds), I made a more conscious effort to preach moderation. Sometimes his response implied that this exchange was a time of reckless abandon, indulging in his every whim, and eventually he would—when he was determined and ready—go cold turkey from his gluttonous habits. I didn't believe him. Everything I witnessed—from excessive eating, to minimal studying, to a basic lack of initiative—seemed to indicate Rafael's lack of discipline.

Once, on a pre-approved student vacation to California, I texted Rafael to confirm his safety en route. This trip, to put it mildly, had already been a point of contention. Up until that time, Rafael had yet to demonstrate the drive, effort, and desire to excel in school, and any day off was cause for celebration. For college-bound students and their parents, missing a week's worth of class time and school work was highly discouraged. Where was the ambitious, overachieving foreign exchange student whom I thought I was getting? Still, I accepted what was.

Hope you arrived safely, I typed into my phone.

Rafael: *Yeah, I'm good. I got here okay.*

I could envision a shirtless, Ray-Banned Rafael lounging poolside, feet up, at a luxurious resort holding some delicious tropical drink, cocktail umbrella included.

Me: *How was your flight?*

Rafael: *It was great. The airport has the best donuts. I got a dozen.*

What? Buying a dozen donuts for our family of five rarely happens, in part because I don't want my kids eating that many. Trust me, we all love a good donut. Just not that many at once, for one person no less. It felt like Rafael was mocking me. I had to dig deep and remember my own childhood, chock-full of candy and cookies, especially when my parents weren't around.

Rafael: *But don't worry, I only ate six. I'll save the other six for later.*

Wow. Unbelievable.

28

But, Is She Nice?

I am not ignorant. I know sex sells. It is a natural act that enables our species to survive.

Depending on what part of the world one is from, different sexual practices, perspectives, and attitudes are considered acceptable. Perhaps others would disagree, but I find people from Latin America to approach sex in a more natural way, as opposed to the overt images and messages I find in the United States. Like the way they move, the way they dance—Latin Americans strike me as more sensual, less raunchy. Nothing feels contrived for the sake of shock value or ticket sales. It's as if it's just part of their ordinary being, a part of their culture, and they know nothing different.

This preconceived notion enabled me to accept the different cultural norms by which I assumed Rafael lived—like the stereotypical skimpy bikinis and Speedo-style men's bathing suits he compared to the "so big" ones he saw at our American beaches (not to mention all the Brazilian topless beaches). I even sensed that lack of parental censorship was attributable to their culture; anything of a sensual or sexual nature was just commonplace. So, although I could understand the differences in what each of us considered acceptable, I still had one battle with Rafael I chose to fight.

In my world, my life, I strive to raise my kids with a healthy respect for what I believe sex should represent. With that goal comes the challenge of often ignoring or contradicting what surrounds us on a daily basis. From music, movies, video games, clothing choices, and even fast food commercials, I frequently offer my opinion to my kids about what I find acceptable and try to guide them according to my beliefs. Having two boys and a girl, the way I present my thoughts to each gender varies. With Alex and Zach, it's about having respect for females, which, in time, translates into meaningful relationships and intimacy, and not viewing them from a strictly superficial level. For Emma, I preach "be classy, not trashy" in behavior and appearance so, hopefully, she attracts those boys who respect and value her.

Hot. The term conjures a certain kind of image regarding one's appearance. As a generous description for an extremely attractive individual, to me, "hot" instills a sexual tone. Though absolutely normal in our culture, it is a label I discourage my kids from using. *Attractive, pretty, handsome, beautiful.* Any of these words suffice, descriptive but seemingly more respectful and less sexually-charged, in my mind.

During Rafael's stay with us, I often sat present and privy to many of the kids' conversations. Frequently in recounting stories of what transpired during their school days, Alex and Rafael would mention students from their shared high school. Very common within these stories would be Rafael's interjection of a "hot" comment.

"Oh, I think I know her. She's hot, right?" or "Is she hot?" he'd ask.

For me, it was like nails on a chalkboard, so I spoke up.

"Rafael, try not to focus on whether a girl is hot or not. Yes, you can appreciate if she is pretty, but the word "hot" to me is so superficial. It's not respectful. Like the only thing you notice in a girl is her looks and that's not how it should be. We live in a world now where women are educated and don't want to be thought of just for what they look like. What matters more is what kind of person she is. Aside from her appearance, is she smart, is she a good person, is she nice?"

Whether he understood or even accepted my viewpoint, I'll never know, but Rafael adopted a new expression.

"She's niiiiiiii-ce," he'd elaborate, drawing it out.

I recognized we were two worlds trying to live as one and, for once, I was able to find some humor in his "compromise."

29

A Brother Like No Other

As much as Emma considered Rafael another brother, his attitude toward and interactions with her differed from Alex and Zach in various ways. He was more tolerant of her, more patient. He was more accepting of her chatterbox, tween-girl ways without the sheer annoyance that Alex and Zach often displayed. Though I know Emma frequently viewed many situations as *them* against *me*, Rafael indulged her in ways neither biological brother would.

One Direction, a popular British all-boy band, reigned supreme in the World According to Emma. Countless 1D magazine cutouts, calendars, posters, souvenir concert tickets, and associated trinkets were pinned, plastered, and mounted in her room. She knew practically every lyric to every song, and she shared many swooning, school-girl fantasies of a happily-ever-after with Harry, Zayn, Louis, Niall, or Liam. One day, with some spare time on her hands, Emma coerced Rafael to join her in producing her latest One Direction creation.

"Rafael, make a video with me!" Emma pleaded, most likely expecting a refusal and subsequent dismissal of her "girlishness."

"What kind of video?"

"Music. I have an app on my phone. Look, we can film ourselves doing whatever."

Emma selected a One Direction song and Rafael acquiesced to her humorously choreographed dance sequences for their video. They moved in unison, their hands, arms, and legs struggling for synchronicity. After multiple rewinds and retakes, their collaborative "What Makes You Beautiful" music video was edited, filtered, and complete.

"Mom, you want to see our video?" Emma asked in an I-really-want-you-to-watch-it appeal.

Emma, Rafael, and I gathered around the small screen.

Their end-product was a keeper, eliciting many laughs, groans, and I-can't-believe-I-just-did-that expressions from Rafael. Emma beamed. She had found a comrade for the afternoon—a very good sport indeed, her brother from another mother.

30
How Sweet It Is

Walmy became Rafael's pet nickname for Walmart, a wonderland representing the veritable bounty that America offers at inexpensive prices.

"Walmy is life. Walmy is my girlfriend," he proclaimed one day, an example of some of the many quirky expressions which developed into what I call Rafael-isms. Over time, they infused much humor into our daily interactions and continue to exist as part of our Overly lingo.

A creature of schedule and habit, I tend to go to our local Walmart Superstore most Sundays after church. It often satisfies my weekly food list and functions as our convenient go-to place.

Rafael frequently desired to accompany me on "Shopping Sundays" at Walmart; it was a chance for him to purchase those things above and beyond what we ordinarily buy for our household.

Upon entering the store one day, I set out to conquer my list. Rafael picked up a shopping basket for himself and followed.

"I'll probably take about forty-five minutes or so to get everything. You want to meet me at the front near the cash registers when you are done?" I asked him.

"Okay, I have to find some things. See you."

Off he went.

Later that day, after unloading all the groceries, I noticed Rafael in the kitchen opening and closing cabinet doors.

"Where can I find a…I don't know what you call it…I'm going to make something, and I need to put it somewhere," he ambiguously explained, gesturing with his palms facing one another two feet apart. After our *Name This Thing* charade-like demonstration concluded, I opened the bottom door of my double oven and Rafael exclaimed, "That's it!" pointing to the layers of baking sheets stacked and stored out of daily sight.

"That's what you're looking for? A baking sheet? What do you need it for?"

"I'm going to make something for all of you. A Brazilian dessert."

I was intrigued.

As I watched him moving about the kitchen, he appeared surprisingly comfortable and knowledgeable. I wondered if his kitchen skills were a byproduct of watching his mother. I admired his gumption.

After some time, Rafael's work neared completion.

"Almost done," he reported, as he rolled some confectionary delight between his buttered-up palms. I eagerly approached the center island, eyeing a couple of baking sheets displaying rows of golf ball-sized, mocha-colored, jimmy-covered treats. *Brigadeiro.* It was the national truffle of Brazil, whose main ingredients of sweetened condensed milk, butter, and chocolate would sabotage any dieter's goal.

"I made them for all of you. Hope you like them." Rafael proudly presented his offering. Not being a true chocolate-lover, I was still floored. Enjoying a bite of the *brigadeiro*, I was practically speechless.

"Wow, they're really good. Thank you so much."

Sweet was the *brigadeiro.* Sweeter was his gesture of thoughtfulness.

31

H-O-R-S-E-ing Around

Through the decade of having lived in our home, we accumulated our share of the traditional outdoor toys and sports apparatuses. Back when we had Rafael, along the back edge of our lawn was a wooden and weathered swing set. To this day, my memories frequently return to our carefree summers of Alex, Zach, Emma, and various neighborhood children enjoying that swing set. Whether navigating the ladder, slide, miniature rock wall, lofted fort, or assorted swings, the kids carved out invaluable childhood moments. On the left side of our lawn was a large soccer net, its white metal frame slightly stained. Having seen its heyday years ago, the soccer goal currently sees infrequent use but continues to adorn our lawn as a perennial fixture. In the front of the house, prior to a home addition being built and the driveway reconfigured, stood our basketball net. Cemented into the ground on the edge of the driveway, the basketball post and hoop saw the most action in its lifetime during Rafael's stay. Whether he ever played before arriving in the US is a moot point. His initial skills revealed he had much to learn in order for his game to improve. Leaping to make a shot, his inaccuracy and lack of agility proved to be quite entertaining, so much so that, over the course of the year, the three boys could be heard frequently laughing during some loose form of a basketball pick-up game.

Over time, Rafael's ball handling and knowledge visibly developed. His repeated exposure to and enjoyment of the game provided a novel and interactive source of physical and mental engagement. Often, the team designations comprised of Alex vs. Zach and Rafael, Alex being the most consistently adept of the three. Occasionally, when game scores still tipped in Alex's favor, the boys discovered ways to even the playing field.

"I know. Alex has to shoot with his weaker side, his left side. And he has to play blindfolded," Zach comically suggested.

Game to the challenge, Alex accepted the new playing conditions. Wearing a red bandana tied around his head to cover his eyes, Alex's sense of balance significantly diminished. I watched them, cringing at the sight of bodies slamming against each other and stumbling onto the driveway. Regardless, the boys had fun, and there were many a day I peeked from behind a dining room window curtain to savor yet another image of the camaraderie shared by the three amigos. Now just memories, I miss those moments and the daily relationship with Rafael we once shared.

Championship games, tournaments, piano and dance recitals often fill our schedules toward the end of an academic year. As much as possible, we attend each of these events as a family in support of one another. On one particular day in May, the six of us assembled ourselves into the car for the drive to Providence where Emma's dance company would be performing their spring recital. As with most theatrical shows, performers typically arrive well before the start of the program. Emma's call time was two hours before showtime. In trying to occupy ourselves, we decided to grab a quick dinner at a pizza parlor in the city. After finishing our meal, we found ourselves with extra time to kill.

"We might as well just drive around for a little since there's no point in getting to the theatre too early," I suggested.

Since the pizza parlor abutted the campus of Brown University, Frank and I thought exploring that area would prove to be of convenience and interest, especially with Alex and Rafael on the cusp of college life. Driving down Thayer Street, the heart of stores and restaurants for Brown students, I enjoyed looking out the window at the hustle and bustle. Unfortunately, but not surprisingly, the three boys were not sharing my appreciation of our drive. Peering over my shoulder, all I could see from my front passenger seat were the tops of their heads and downcast eyes. They remained engrossed in the latest music, movie, or video game on each of their phones.

"Hey, guys, let's put your electronics away and use this time to look out the windows. It's not healthy to always be on your phones; it's time to disconnect. It's a beautiful day. Use this time to look around, see what's going on around you, talk to one another and interact. I'm sure there will be time later to relax with your phones."

Begrudgingly, and with the expected teenager eye-roll, Alex, Zach, and Rafael turned off their screens.

"I love watching people. I think it's interesting to try to figure out what they're about. Like, where are they from, what is their story?" I attempted to spur their imaginations. "For example, look over there," I directed, pointing to a couple standing under a budding tree outside of an academic building. "What's up with them? Do you think they're friends? Or do you think they're a couple? Maybe they're just in the initial flirting stage, or maybe they're already boyfriend and girlfriend?" I hypothesized, reflecting on mine and Frank's blossoming relationship as freshmen at Bucknell University. Almost immediately, Rafael's forthrightness practically paralyzed us.

"No, that's impossible, they're not a couple. She's too Asian."

I was dumbfounded.

"What did you say?" all four of us demanded.

"The boy is white, and the girl is too Asian. Nah, they couldn't be a couple."

Each of us practically pummeled him with a verbal barrage.

"What do you mean, too Asian?"

"Rafael, you can't say something like that. That's so racist."

"Look around, Rafael, you are sitting in a car with a family that includes three Asian people and a white guy. You have been living with us for almost a year and that's what you think?"

Feeling attacked, Rafael became defensive. "What's wrong with what I said? There's nothing wrong with it. It's true. She's too Asian."

Trying to diffuse the situation, Frank and I calmly attempted to explain our perception.

"Rafael, in our country, we have a lot of racial diversity. There are also a lot of mixed couples, and we're one of them. When you say something like 'too Asian,' it implies something negative. Like there's something wrong. You wouldn't walk into a place full of Asian people, say something like that, and come out without probably being beaten up. It sounds so racist."

"Well, I'm not a racist," Rafael declared.

"Okay, we'd like to think you're not, but you have to realize, in our world, you just don't go around saying something like that. It sounds terrible and it's not politically correct."

"I'm not a racist," he adamantly repeated.

Approaching Emma's showtime, we headed toward the theatre. In the few minutes between this heated exchange and arriving at the parking lot, all had gone quiet in the car.

The lights in the theatre dimmed soon after we took a row of seats, and the recital commenced. The boys sat in stone-cold silence. Even during the brief pauses between the dance numbers, when patrons would share their whispered opinions, I noticed zero interaction between Alex, Zach, and Rafael.

When intermission came, the audience was invited into the lobby for refreshments. By the time we fell in line to purchase a snack, it dawned on me that Rafael was not with us.

"Where is Rafael?" I asked.

"Who knows? He's mad. He's not talking to us."

I quickly scanned the crowd and spotted Rafael sitting alone to the side of the concession room, eating brownies in solitude. This wasn't the time or the place to address anything, and time was probably the best thing for all of us to de-escalate.

After getting home that evening, I approached Rafael, attempting to extend an olive branch and provide an explanation, one that he could hopefully understand.

"Rafael, it's hard to explain, but when you say something is too *anything*, it paints a negative picture. Like there's a point where, if you pass it, that thing is no longer a good thing…like too salty, or too skinny, or too cold."

"So, what should I have said?"

"I'm not sure. But saying 'too Asian' definitely sounds racist, so you shouldn't say that. Even if you truly think it, you can't go around saying that, at least not with us." I found myself spinning in circles, the most appropriate and enlightening word choice eluding me. Searching his face for any glimpse of understanding, I couldn't help but justify my position with the remembrance that this was an exchange year. Promoting tolerance, understanding, and acceptance of different cultures and people was central to the mission of any exchange. Finally, after a few seconds, Rafael displayed a lightbulb moment.

"Oh, I know! Next time I'll just say *very* Asian."

Ugh. I conceded to yet another stalemate.

The next morning was Mother's Day, another commercially-driven Hallmark holiday, but possibly the one annual day children pay an obligatory tribute to their moms. In our family, our kids present me with small gifts of appreciation, albeit a tradition we established with Frank's guidance (and likewise, mine for Father's Day). For me, truly, the actual gifts never mean as much as the thought behind their handmade cards. Not only do they save money, but their real value is in the expression of their feelings that help diffuse the countless days of me feeling maternally inadequate. Often feeling taken for granted and beaten down as a mother many days of the year and second-guessing my efforts, I do eagerly anticipate Mother's Day. With the hope that Alex, Zach, and Emma will somehow convey my worth in their own way, I look for confirmation that they really do appreciate me. Is that an insecurity? Yes, but it's reassuring to know I possess the kind of relationship with my children that I'm aspiring toward daily. On that particular Mother's Day, I awoke to a display of gifts and cards propped up on the kitchen counter.

"Why don't you open your cards and gifts?" Frank prompted as I prepared my morning cup of coffee, all four kids gathered around the center island. Rafael's anger from the night before seemed to have dissipated, and the normal, playful energy between all four kids felt restored. As I read through each card, I had a smile on my face and in my heart. Even Rafael's card was poignant, expressing gratitude for all I had done for him during his exchange year. We had come a long way since his Thanksgiving essay, and he had surely progressed in his English writing skills. After I thanked all of them, the kids dispersed to get ready for church. When Frank and I were finally alone in the kitchen, Frank had a perplexed look on his face, his eyes squinting in confusion.

"Did you read Rafael's card?"

"I did, you saw me, I read all of the cards."

"Did you read *all* of it?"

"I think so. Or at least I thought I did. Why?"

"Read it again. Read the very bottom. The last line. Maybe you didn't see it."

I opened Rafael's card and re-read it, searching for whatever Frank was referring to. There it was. On the very bottom of the card, in the smallest font his computer would produce, I read the words that, upon first glance, resembled a smudged line and therefore were overlooked.

"I ain't no racist."

Double ugh.

33

AβC

Playing the piano was a given for me and my brother during our childhood, as it was for all my cousins who lived in our town. Auntie Amelia, my mother's sister, was our piano teacher, and I always believed we had to play the piano in order to provide my aunt with students. Now I realize the error in my thinking. Yes, we had to play, but for the reason that it's just what my family did. Some were architects, some painted, some played multiple instruments, some danced, some sculpted bonsai trees, but all played the piano. Artistry was in our blood.

Truthfully, I hated the piano. Or maybe it was the practicing I despised. I have vivid memories of pretending to practice, banging out notes without any care of improving or correcting any mistakes. I didn't see the point in piano lessons, and I questioned if its perceived lack of worth justified the cost. Year after year, at the annual recital, my heart felt like it would explode out of my chest from nerves, and I couldn't understand why my parents would force such cruel and unjust punishment on me. Over time, however, my name began to creep its way down the list on the recital program, the more advanced students' names toward the end. Still, regardless of any sense of accomplishment, I failed to appreciate how playing the piano benefitted me.

It's ironic that when Frank and I had kids, it was a no-brainer that piano lessons were a requirement. Initially, it was for making them better-rounded. But, my insistence that they each play the piano has definitely come with its share of battles regarding adequate practice time. The benefits of a musical background are unquantifiable but, to me, very real. A developing ear and appreciation for an art, a physical skill promoting dexterity and fine motor ability, a cognitive challenge that taps into a different part of their brains which would otherwise possibly lay dormant.

Upon Rafael joining our family, he soon discovered how the piano sat centrally in our home and how practice time ranked high on my priority list in our kids' daily schedules. He witnessed my consistent urgings for Alex, Zach, and Emma to coordinate their daily routines to accommodate the sharing of the inherited forty-year-old upright Everett from my childhood. As Zach begrudgingly positioned himself on the bench to practice one day, dislike segued into diversion.

"Rafael, I should teach you how to play the piano," Zach suggested.

"Really? Is it hard?" Rafael's curiosity was aroused.

"Come over here, I'll teach you. We can start piano lessons, so you learn to play."

Though I typically get irritated by Zach's lack of focus and initiative during practice time, this "arrangement" of teaching Rafael earned my respect in both him as the student and Zach as a teacher.

"First, you need to know that this is middle C," Zach indicated by pressing down on a centrally-located ivory key. "The keys are like the alphabet, going from A to G. They're arranged in what is called octaves, made of eight notes, and the pattern just repeats so the keyboard has a bunch of octaves." After pecking out an octave in demonstration, Zach encouraged Rafael to mimic him, to acquire the fundamental ABC's of the piano. I peeked around the corner of the kitchen, amused by the sight.

"Get up for a second. I need to find something." Zach lifted the hinged lid of the wooden bench. Searching through the variety of music books, he unearthed what was possibly our kids' very first book of piano songs.

"Let's try this. C-D-E," Zach cajoled.

Processing how each written note corresponded to a specific key on the keyboard, Rafael listened intently, mentally connecting the notes written on paper to the keys beneath his fingers. Zach began bridging the cognitive with the physical, first demonstrating the foundational ABC's of the right hand, as well as the left. After reviewing the first two songs of the book, Zach finished the first lesson.

"Okay, so now you have to practice these two songs for the next time. You did a good job."

Rafael's smile was filled with humor and pride.

Zach and Rafael's piano lessons persisted throughout the year, albeit with regular irregularity, but sufficient to the point where, by late spring, Rafael had attempted the majority of the songs in his beginner book. When an AFS email announced their final social event for that year, the host families in our region were invited to an appreciation dinner. In addition to asking each of the students to provide a native, prepared food dish to share, the program's staff also requested their participation in a talent show.

"Uh oh. I don't have a talent, what am I going to do?" Rafael contemplated, unsure of the true seriousness of this petition.

"You can play the piano," Zach advocated.

"Are you serious? I don't really know how to play. I just learned this year."

"Yeah. But I don't think anyone is expecting anything big. More just an opportunity to participate. It'll be great. You can show everyone what you learned over the year," I encouraged.

In April, gathered together in the parish hall of a church, host families and exchange students convened for our farewell appreciation dinner. A bounty of various ethnic foods was enjoyed by all as we sat in anticipation of the talent show. When the time arrived, eager students bravely ascended the steps leading up to a stage spanning the width of one of the parish hall's walls.

"This is going to be fun," I remarked to Alysa, our neighbor who hosted Camille, a French girl, for the year. Sitting across from one another at our banquet table, she inquired, "What is Rafael doing for his talent?"

"Zach taught him how to play the piano."

"Really?"

"Yup. Just wait."

After a parade of talent, it was Rafael's turn. Alysa and I shared an exchange of smiles, nervous for him. Taking his position on the piano bench, his back toward the audience and poised for his musical debut, Rafael enlisted the help of a page-turner. He had practiced two songs with Zach—"Canoe Song" to be his second, complete with dyads (two notes played simultaneously together) and an alternating arrangement of notes between both hands. For some, perhaps a Bach or Beethoven piece was expected. For others, especially those with any musical knowledge, they more likely sat impressed with the courage Rafael possessed, putting his newly-developed ability on full display. Despite a few mistakes, he plugged through his songs. Unbeknownst to him, he played like a pro. Not in quality, but in the fact that he concealed his wrong notes. He never stopping playing and ignored any mistakes, a skill groomed in seasoned performers. Rafael concluded to a round of thunderous applause.

"Wow, I give him credit. That was brave," Alysa praised. Frank, the kids, and I laughed in disbelief and absolute amazement.

Rounding out the evening's festivities, after the talent show portion ended, staff members beckoned for the exchange students to assemble on stage to express a few words of gratitude for their host families. Several students cried, conveying the heartfelt range of emotions experienced during their year abroad, including the love they felt toward their American families. I had no idea what to expect from Rafael, who was ordinarily unexpressive in terms of affection.

"I'd like to thank the Overlys, my American family, for being so nice and letting me live with them. I love you all," he timidly articulated. In that moment, I wasn't sure if he was following suit, parroting similar sentiments of the students preceding him. Regardless, goosebumps rose from my skin. I had a hard time looking him in the eye—mental snippets of our year's struggles and highlights floating in my brain; it was bittersweet. We had made it through, and soon it would be done. Our exchange year, our time as a family of six was coming to a close. I swallowed hard, a feeble attempt to keep the tears in my eyes from falling.

34

A Tale of Two Families

As we began to wind down our year together, AFS had finally approved Rafael's family's visit. Leslie, Wilton, and Giovanna were scheduled to arrive at the end of May and stay for approximately a week and a half. We were excited to meet them and observe their dynamics. To welcome them, I gathered a sampling of local attraction brochures and edible staples—granola bars, nuts, crackers, chocolate—and packaged them with a short note in a gift basket, ready to greet them in their hotel room upon their arrival. Within their first few days, we shared several friendly meals and were entertained by the language barrier, relying on Rafael, Google Translate, and charade-like gestures to communicate.

Understandably, Rafael's family wanted to spend every minute with him. To a degree, I get it. If it had been a reunion with my child, I'd feel the same. However, from our host family standpoint, with several AFS "rules" being violated but supposedly approved by the organization (a situation blamed on the contradictions between AFS USA and AFS Paraguay), their trip was not without issues. Some were small inconveniences, others seemed to disregard and undermine what I believed to be vital aspects of the exchange year. Like when Rafael's family prematurely picked him up from a mandatory, overnight AFS retreat meant as a time for staff and students to congregate and share their experiences and insights. Rafael's early dismissal minimized his opportunity to engage. Though I resented his exemption, it wasn't my place to enforce his full attendance.

Approximately a week into their visit, after many mornings, afternoons, and evenings of his parents monopolizing his time, hurt and bitterness took hold.

"Mom, I don't get it," Zach began. "I mean, I understand they missed him and want to spend time with him, but he's only with us for another month. Then they get him for the rest of their lives."

Rafael had occupied that niche in Zach's life, somewhere between brother and great friend, someone to laugh with, play with, and share everything with—minus the sibling rivalry. It was an unending sleepover where inside jokes helped form an intangible bond among all four kids.

"Yeah, I know. It bugs me too. I don't think they see things that way," I played devil's advocate.

When Alex and Emma also expressed similar feelings, my communication-is-best personality sparked me to write a letter to Leslie and Wilton. Knowing I could express myself more thoroughly and rationally in written form, I capitalized on several situations to convey our hurt. Asking to speak with Leslie, using Rafael's ability to translate my request, I gestured to make themselves comfortable on the family room sectional. I could hear Wilton, Alex, and Zach immersed in a basketball game on the driveway and decided it was best to communicate mother to mother. Rafael, Leslie, and Giovanna sat side by side, unaware of the nature of this summons. Occasionally, Rafael snuggled up to Leslie, his head resting between her jawline and shoulder. Reading my letter line by line, I trusted Rafael's translation to capture the essence of my message. I observed Leslie's face for any visible empathy but feared my words might elicit a knee-jerk reaction. Based on my letter, Rafael explained how we, as a family, felt dismissed once they arrived. That we had been entrusted with his care for the year, and that we had grown to include him as part of our family. That our remaining time together was limited.

After all was said on my behalf, Rafael switched gears to translate Leslie's response. Even before hearing him speak, I sensed her compassion. I saw it in her eyes. There was respect—respect for all we had done for her son. Respect for how challenging the exchange process was for everyone, themselves included. Respect for our feelings. I had given my all, parenting Rafael like my own, caring about what kind of person he grew into. I felt I owed it to myself for my truth to be told. It could have been a missed opportunity, to allow their trip to come and go with the harboring of ill will, but it turned out to be a chance for both of us mothers to explain our views and reconcile our emotions. It added a deeper layer to our exchange, never anticipated, but invaluable all the same.

35

What's in a Name?

Mom Overly. That's what I call my mother-in-law. Not *Bubba*, not *Nanay,* as family tradition would have dictated. Not *Mother Overly,* either, since my perceived formality of that name didn't exude the familiarity or closeness I wanted to convey. From the start of our marriage, *Mom Overly* became the chosen name.

I imagine that foreign exchange students grapple with a similar challenge, both mentally and emotionally. Knowing that a similar name, a label, doesn't in any way substitute, minimize, or betray their loyalties to their natural family, but feeling that perhaps it does. And so, from the beginning of our exchange year, we broached the Name Game

issue with Rafael. Per AFS suggestions, Frank and I encouraged him to call us by whatever he preferred. Comically, this resulted in him not calling us by any name at all. If ever he needed our attention, his default approach was to just speak. In regard to Alex, Zach, and Emma, Rafael dubbed them "(Sexy) Lexi," "Sackie," and "Emo." Conversely, they nicknamed him "Rash."

Such a strange thing, to not be called anything. If ever I took it personally, I no longer do. I've since realized that I do not need a specific name to label our relationship because the experiences we shared with Rafael can't be conveyed, encapsulated, or qualified in a single name. I know what I know, and I feel what I feel—and that is good enough. So really, what's the point?

36

A Memory's Keeper

Time frequently dulls, changes, or sometimes erases the memories that form much of a person's history. Countless things can trigger those memories. For me, specific sights, smells, concepts, and words often weave Rafael right back into the fibers of our daily life. A particular scent of AXE body spray. A burger with bacon and BBQ sauce on a menu. Ronda Rousey. Fudge. "Ain't." Anything and everything Brazilian.

Selfishly, I wanted to gift him those images and memories of our six-member family and all that we shared. Unaware of my intention, Rafael posed for innumerable photo opportunities that depicted a year in the

life as an Overly. In the form of a photo album, I hoped this gift would be a fitting, concrete, and lasting vehicle in which his memories could be accessed.

On Rafael's final night, the five of us presented him gifts. An obscene supply of Pop-Tarts and Reese's Peanut Butter Cups, a football, and a Rhode Island-themed Christmas ornament—just to name a few. Purposely waiting until the end, I finally bestowed the photo album.

"Here you go. It's the last one."

"Ooh, what is it?"

"Open it. You'll see. I hope you like it."

Removing the last of the wrapping paper, Rafael skimmed his fingers over the cover. Flipping through page after page, he remained speechless, re-visiting his year's experiences.

"Oh my gosh. How did you…? I mean, I knew you took a lot of pictures, but I had no idea. And look, they're in…. I don't how you say it."

I chuckled. "Rafael, you know me better than that. Do you think it's a coincidence that they're in chronological order?"

He sat, enthralled by the visual timeline. Several images had been captured unbeknownst to him, eliciting laughter for the goofy, happy, and fun memories recollected.

"Hopefully, now you won't forget us. And you can show your family everything you did over the year."

"This is awesome."

A great end to a great year.

"Rafael, we're going to be leaving soon," I called out to him the next morning, as he packed his final belongings. Helping him load everything into the car, we questioned if any last-minute shuffling of suitcase contents would be necessary, given the airline's weight restrictions for checked baggage.

"It'll be okay. I can't help it, I have too much stuff. If I have to pay extra, that's fine."

"All right. Do you have everything?" I could hardly believe that in a few short hours we would be dropping him off so he could begin his trek back home.

"I think so. If not, oh well. All the important stuff is in here," Rafael tapped his carry-on bag. "Computer, PlayStation, and my album."

Shock. That was the only way to describe the pleasant surprise. His album was sandwiched between his most-prized possessions. In the spectrum melding black and white, and all of the grays in between, this was by far a brightest of whites moment.

37

And Then There Were Five

Our Toyota SUV circled the parking lot, searching for a vacant spot near the drop-off point. Rafael possessed excess baggage compared to the other students, which required each of us to pitch in to unload the car. After signing him in, the reality of parting ways fully hit us. There were exhibitions of affection and nostalgia between host families and students. Some were laughing, some were crying. Some stood in a lingering embrace.

Not wanting to prolong the inevitable, we gathered in our own separate bubble, Rafael at its center.

"So, I guess this is it," I began.

"It's been great, Rafael. We'll see you again," the kids assuredly stated.

Melancholy gripped us all as each of them and Frank shared a final, awkward hug with him, hoping our futures would eventually intersect and reconnect us.

Then he turned to me.

"It was great having you, Rafael, it really was. I hope you enjoyed it. I hope you learned some things."

"I did. And I want you to keep teaching me."

Ugh. But this time it felt different—a guttural sensation infused with wistfulness. I swallowed hard, allowing the tears to fall as we walked back to the car as a family of five.

Aware of Rafael's return itinerary, I waited to reach out. I remained cognizant that he needed to reacclimate to his former world, people included, and begin to disconnect from all of us. After a few days had passed, I sent him a text to ensure he had arrived safely.

Me: *How was your trip?*

Rafael: *Long. After you dropped me off, they took all the students to some amusement park for the day.*

Me: *Really? I didn't know that. We thought you were just going to a hotel or airport.*

Rafael: *I know. And it was soooo hot. Like 95 degrees.*

LOL. In attempting to cram all his belongings into his luggage, Rafael thought it best to wear some of his heavier pieces to avoid packing them. I could picture him in a park somewhere, covered head to toe in a sweatshirt, leather jacket, jeans, and construction boots.

Rafael: *I was melting.*

The humor punctuated the grand finale of this exchange year.

Me: *Well, hopefully, it was still fun. I just wanted to check in with you, make sure you got home safely. How is it being back?*

Rafael: *Weird. Like when I got on the plane and realized it was over. Then when I got home and took a shower. It was just weird.*

Me: *I suppose that's expected. It'll be an adjustment again, but you'll be fine. Tell your family we said hi, we'll talk soon.*

Now, armed with the knowledge he was back in his mother's good hands, it was my time to detach. Mentally, I needed to return to being a mother of three. Just as we had welcomed him into our lives, it was now time to let go and move forward, re-establishing our family dynamics. Despite Rafael's absence, I knew our relationship was entering a new phase, not ending. What seeded during the year took root in our lives and grew into an arrangement of petals and leaves—a beautiful, heart-shaped, Brazilian Petunia.

What I have come to appreciate from this *intercambio* is that we have all grown and continue to do so. I am less quick to judge and more apt to ponder another point of view, recognizing the role of a person's history, influences, and circumstances in a given situation. I have an enriched sensitivity for those needing assistance—"You're a sucker for foreigners," as my kids say. Even Leslie and Wilton's ability to endure Rafael's exchange helped frame my perspective when Alex left for college. That is something none of us could have ever predicted, that Rafael would be my teacher, as well. Our AFS adventure was defined by working through the blacks, savoring the whites, but cemented by the grays of every day. To this day, and moving forward, our interactions will tint my mindset. It was, in the truest sense of the word, an exchange—a gift that keeps on giving.

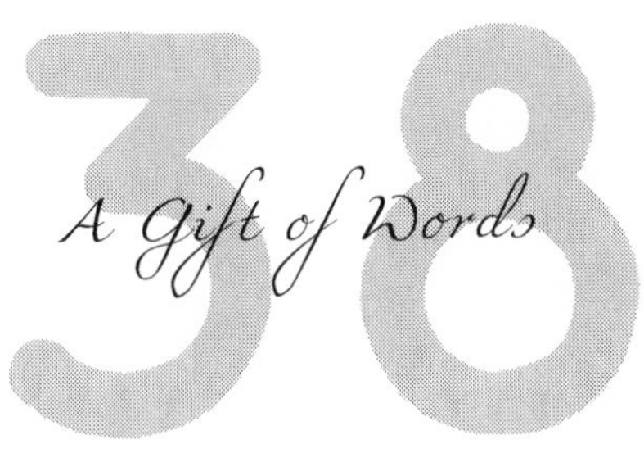

38
A Gift of Words

(From Wilton José Gabas, Jr., 6/11/14)

Translated as intended:

First, I want to thank each one of you, including Lola (your mother), for the warm welcome you provided. The reception and lunch were unforgettable, truly unforgettable. I imagine the work it took, especially in getting those giant lobsters for us to enjoy…very special!!!

I know Leslie already sent a thank-you email on our behalf, but I would like to comment on something particular and quite objective…

During our family gatherings, I observed what mattered to me…the affection that you have for Rafa, and I also managed to see the affection he has for you. For a father and mother to let a child live with an unknown family, in another country, is very worrying, as it was for me and Leslie. It was a very delicate phase for all of us, and I imagine for Rafa as well. Yet over time, we came to trust each other. We observed behaviors, attitudes and small details that showed us your values. It was not easy for us at first, but with each passing day, we began to feel more comfortable, peaceful and secure in the family.

We discovered how much all of you—Hannah, Frank, Alex, Zach (fireman, my partner in basketball) and super-nice Emma—are "Spices," educated, religious, affectionate.

It's hard to say thank you with words. You participated in my teenage son's year of growth and adolescence. Importantly, you

added concepts of life, education, and respect that complement our teachings, and I know that they will never be forgotten! I also saw the great dedication as if Rafa were a son: Frank taught him how to ride a bike, very exciting! You showed him sports such as skiing and many others that we do not have in our tropical climate and transformed his dream into a wonderful and unforgettable reality…I love you very much!

We know you had to make changes in your daily lives, including the fact that one of the children slept in another room to leave a room just for Rafa. That was a big sacrifice that gave him a lot of privacy and comfort….

I apologize to you, Hannah, Frank, and also the children for inconveniences we caused during our visit and how everyone's routine changed. But we could not take it anymore. Our trip had already been discussed and authorized by AFS here in Paraguay. In a very conscious way, I have to admit that in some respect, the program is right. But you also have to understand that we, as parents, really missed our child!

We are arriving at the end of the program, and I see what Rafa was at the beginning and what he has become now. We owe a great deal to all of you. Always know that you have a family in Paraguay and Brazil with open doors to welcome you with affection and gratitude…And, Hannah, especially for you, the thank you is bigger because I know as a mother you took care of my son as if he was your own. I understand that it has not been easy to adapt for everyone but you all succeeded with great success!

I also want you to know that Rafa loves each of you…you became a great family!!! I have great and eternal affection for all of you…a big kiss on everyone's heart. Thank you so much!

~Wilton

Note: I mean this very professionally and with a lot of seriousness. Despite some discomforts I had personally, and despite being annoyed by the staff of AFS for the sake of communication between AFS Paraguay and AFS United States, I'm very happy with the result of the program. I really do not know where you could have found a family so wonderful and so special to take care of my son as if he were family. The Overlys: Mr. Frank, Mrs. Hannah, and their children Alex, Zach, and Emma—a blessed family and huge heart.

Congratulations AFS for meeting people like the Overly family. Congratulations!!!

39

One Year Later

Rafael's discipline improved dramatically after completing his exchange program. When he returned home, he launched a self-initiated crusade of actualization. The Reese's and Pop-Tarts were substituted with a regular diet of healthier choices such as broiled chicken and brown rice. He started exercising at his local gym religiously. He swapped his former habits of late-night video games with a more responsible and productive sleep schedule. He continued his education, the ultimate goal being acceptance into a reputable, Brazilian university for medical school. Done. (And, he ranked #9 out of 10,000 admitted students based on entrance exam scores.) When he sent me a picture one day of his apartment's study area, the caption read: *Look at the organization*! Was this the same Rafael I'd asked to organize his school binders, tidy up his workspace at our kitchen table, and apply himself in school? The differences were remarkable.

Rafael returned to visit us one year after his departure. In that time span, we communicated regularly through texting or Skype. Alex, Zach, Emma, and Rafael often coordinated their schedules to connect, considering the time difference between our respective countries. As Rafael's trip neared, the kids excitedly created a bucket list of every restaurant meal and activity that needed to be enjoyed during his stay.

"Five Guys, for sure," Rafael pitched, a burger his go-to American comfort food.

"And Moe's," Zach added, referring to their southwest burritos.

"Ooh, yeah. Remember their queso?" Rafael recalled. Permitting a hiatus from his strict diet during the upcoming vacation, he mentally prepared himself.

"But it's okay. We'll play lots of basketball so we're not just eating."

"And we have to do our annual family bike ride."

When Rafael finally arrived, the four kids easily filled the time reliving favorite pastimes: basketball, video games, bonfires, movies, eating s'mores, and simply being together. Doing anything.

Doing nothing. But enjoying themselves all the same. There was a natural rhythm that easily surfaced from our family of six.

Sitting around the kitchen table for dinner during his return, I was curious about Rafael's perception of things from his exchange year.

"So, Rafael, what do you think is the biggest difference between then and now? Now that you've had time to go back home and compare things, what do you think? Like, do you think you learned anything?"

His index finger rested on his lips. "That's a good question. I think I learned a lot of things, I was so messed up before," Rafael said, using his natural catch-all Rafaelism for describing such things. Truly, some awareness had occurred. And though I realize time and maturity would have naturally grown him as well, I think it's fair to say that everything he experienced during his exchange year helped enhance his development. Not just in his way of doing things, but in his way of thinking.

Driving Rafael to the airport at the end of his visit, Frank and I engaged him in light conversation, reminiscing about the highlights of his trip. We were at the tail-end of a vacation, our annual reunion in Deep Creek, Maryland. The house we historically rented for the week was perched lakeside with direct access to the water. Rafael's week-long grin indicated his enjoyment, tubing possibly his favorite activity.

Prior to our Maryland trip, during the first half of Rafael's visit, our family set out on our traditional summer bike ride. We retraced the route that, only one year before, Rafael had managed without any difficulties. It was a sensory-rich path, the main road hugging the ocean views. Seagulls swooped, waves roared against the shoreline, and the air occasionally smelled like fish. Riding caboose, I had a vantage point of ensuring we all rode together in a tidy, compact line. Frank led the way, followed by the kids, listening for my sudden burst of "Car!" It's no surprise I served as the primary lookout for potential hazards. I also instructed the kids to maintain a safe distance from one another and discouraged any antics—zig-zagging, hands-free riding, the typical stunts—in case Rafael tried to copy them. It was a relatively flat route, allowing our ride to be more about enjoyment and less about effort. Occasionally, however, there were slight hills with the descents.

"Rafael, if you're going uphill, sometimes it's easier if you stand up a little while you pedal. Then, when you are…" my words failed to come out quickly enough as Rafael crested a hill and the momentum carried him out of earshot and downward—fast.

"Make sure you brake as you go down!" I yelled.

Within a split second, Rafael was upright on his bike, then down on the ground. My brain tried to catch up as Emma and I frantically approached.

"Rafael, are you okay?"

"I think so," he responded, assessing the abrasions on his knee and the palms of his hands.

What first appeared as ashen streaks of road rash soon transformed into miniature wells of blood breaking the surface of his skin. Emma and I grimaced at the sight. I hollered to get Frank and the boys to return. Explaining to Frank we had no bandages at our disposal, and no convenience store nearby, we used Alex's extra, clean T-shirt to wrap around Rafael's handlebars. We hoped that applying pressure through his palms would stanch the blood and provide some temporary coverage and pain relief.

"Do you think you can keep riding?" Frank asked.

"Yeah, I should be okay." His classic stoicism was always a favorable feature. I doubted whether any of my kids would have been as calm.

"Okay, so let's keep going a few more miles to where we normally stop for food. There are some stores there. Maybe we can buy some first-aid stuff there."

Rafael gingerly mounted his bike and we resumed our ride, but this time caution and concern were more pronounced. When we approached the plaza, it became obvious that no one sold the items we sought.

"Wait here," I commanded the bunch. Entering a stationary store, I prayed for sympathy.

"Excuse me, do you have any Band-Aids we can use? I'm happy to pay for them," I asked the woman standing behind the cash register. "My family was on a bike ride and our exchange student fell, and now he's bleeding."

She followed me out of the store as I spoke, both of us noticing a random passerby speaking to Frank and the kids. He observed our situation from a distance and volunteered to search his car for anything that might be of use. Seeing Rafael's hands, the store owner finally comprehended our intentions and she sprang into action.

"Well, I don't have any Band-Aids, but I can give you a bunch of paper towels and tape," she said as she scurried back into the store and headed for the closet-sized, not-for-the-public restroom. "Here, he can come in and rinse his hands off while I get some tape."

By then, the kind gentleman returned from his vehicle, antibacterial ointment in hand. Frank thanked him, then prompted Rafael to head to the bathroom. After running cold water over his hands, we fashioned mummy-like coverings. Though not ideal, we were grateful for this temporary solution and thanked the owner for her assistance. As we stood outside of the store contemplating our next move, Rafael and I acknowledged the selflessness of these strangers.

"You don't have to, but maybe it would be thoughtful to write a thank-you note to that woman and we can mail it to her. I'm sure she's not expecting it."

He agreed.

"Yeah. They were both so nice. And they really didn't have to help."

Proud of the humanity extended toward Rafael, I couldn't help but wonder how the same scenario would have played out in Brazil. Would locals have stepped in to help? Would they turn a blind eye? I'm not sure. In the past, Rafael had described a prevailing keep-to-yourself mentality about his home country. Simple acts of compassion sounded rare, at least outside of immediate family and friends. But in that moment, I hoped Rafael saw the beauty in helping others unconditionally. It was a far better lesson for him than anything I could have preached. God bless America.

"Yeah, that's too bad you fell on our bike ride. That was kind of scary," I recalled Rafael's healing hands. "And it made tubing kind of hard for you to hold on, huh?"

"That's okay, they'll be fine."

We drove out of Maryland and into Pennsylvania, headed for the Pittsburgh airport where Rafael would catch his return flight home. Finding new topics to discuss, I inquired about how his family was doing. I wondered if there were any developments in their attempt at selling their store with the hope of moving back to Brazil.

"I don't think they're going to sell it for a while. The business is doing well and so they'll probably stay in Paraguay. They're actually thinking of opening new stores."

"Really? Do you think they'll stay a long time?" I wondered.

"I'm not sure. But my mom has talked about eventually moving to the US. Maybe Miami. She likes it in Florida."

"Seriously? I thought you all wanted to go back to Brazil."

"Things aren't great there, so you never know."

"What would you do then? Stay in Paraguay? I know you want to go to a university in Brazil, but what about after? What if your parents moved to the US? What would you do? Would you actually consider living here?"

Brazil is the best place in the whole world, there's no other place I'd rather be….

His words from his Thanksgiving essay never left me.

"I would. I do like Florida." It was Rafael's first outward concession that he would consider a different country as a viable residence.

"Would you ever think about applying to college here in the States? I mean, if you don't get into medical school back home? We would be closer to each other then."

"I think so. That would be cool. But it's so expensive here for college. In Brazil, if I get into a program, it's free. That's why it's so competitive. We'll see…."

I'm not sure when Rafael's outlook changed. Maybe it was during his exchange year. Maybe it was when he returned home and had something to compare it to. From this conversation (and additional future ones), I inferred an open-mindedness in him that didn't previously exist. In an odd way, I took partial ownership for that. Perhaps his exchange really did have a positive impact after all.

EPILOGUE

The Story Continues

Rafael left two weeks ago. It had been two years since we last saw him after his first return visit. During that time, he moved back to Brazil to start medical school, living independently in an apartment.

Naturally, we were all very excited to be reunited. Weeks prior to his departure from Brazil, however, our anticipation fizzled. The Brazilian government had imposed a recent suspension of issuing passports because of a budget crisis, and Rafael needed to renew his.

"Oh man, are you kidding? That's so dumb." Zach was forlorn, his evolving maturity boomeranged right back to his Eeyore tendencies.

"All we can do is wait and see. It's out of our control," I encouraged.

With the passport situation in effect, Rafael and his family made alternate arrangements and drove seven hours to Paraguay, hoping to get a new one there.

After a few days, my phone dinged.

Rafael: I got it! I got my passport from Paraguay!

We were thrilled.

Rafael's stay was for a week and a half in August. His birthday, however, was in July. We never had the chance to celebrate it with him, and even cards or gifts were infrequently sent—the mail system in South America does not guarantee safe or timely delivery.

In preparing for his first meal with us, I decided to celebrate his birthday in a traditional Overly way. I shopped for gifts, seeking ones I thought would be fitting and personal. One was a small, stone-carved elephant figurine, its spirit animal representing strength and pride. One was a tiger's eye beaded bracelet, similar to the one Alex wears, a look I find cool on guys. Another gift was a Swiss Army pocket knife. Compared to the one I use, its convenient size makes it ideal to suspend from a keychain. Imagining scenes of Rafael walking across a darkened campus alone at night, prepared to ward off attackers, the mother in me wanted to include a gift of function and utility. We also gifted him stickers for his laptop, following the current teenager trend of marking their gadgets with ideas, words, or images. One sticker, a red, white, and blue shield with a white star represented Captain America, a nod to Rafael and Zach's shared love of anything Marvel. A second sticker read: *Rash.* I thought it was hilarious. Another gift included two baseball hats, one with "RI" on the front, the other with the Steelers logo, our household maintaining its allegiance to its Pittsburgh roots. My final present for Rafael was to be a small, framed picture collage, assembled from our upcoming slew of selfies and candid photos.

True to form, my plan was to gift it as a surprise on his last night with us.

The mother in me also wanted to make a special treat for his birthday. After considering several options, I focused on dulce de leche, a caramel-like staple in Rafael's culture. I found a recipe for dulce de leche cheesecake, grateful for its relative ease and how well it generally turned out.

On the day of Rafael's arrival, Alex requested the day off from work to accompany me to Boston Logan International Airport. The morning traffic was reasonable, so we found ourselves arriving early. Unfortunately, Rafael soon texted us to say he missed his last plane departing Newark, the fourth and final leg of his journey. *Four planes? Boy, he must really want to see us.*

When the time finally arrived for Rafael's plane to land, Alex and I waited at the arriving passengers' security point. After thirty minutes of many double-takes and mistaken sightings, Rafael emerged from the stream of deboarding passengers. In a way, he was the same Rafael. But he was a young man now. I approached him with a hug, surprised at how it truly felt like I was welcoming one of my own after a prolonged absence. He gave me the slightest of pecks on the cheek. It resembled one of those automatic displays of familial affection upon greeting one another, free of any hesitation. I was flattered.

We chatted almost the entire way back to Rhode Island, including a lunch break at Qdoba. Rafael was starving, having been traveling for more than twenty-four hours. While eating, we talked about medical school and his apartment, his family, and his new girlfriend, Juliana.

"I never expected to meet someone this soon, not someone I like this much. I was so surprised," Rafael shared as we each devoured our burritos. I, too, was surprised. Just a week before, he had casually mentioned to Alex that he had been with more than thirty girls within a month of starting medical school.

What?!

"I mean, I met some really pretty girls, but something feels different with Juliana. She's in medical school, too, but different than mine."

"So, she's smart. That's good."

"And she's nice. Really. It's so easy to talk to her, comfortable. And I really like her voice, it's so cute."

Teasing him about the myriad of girls I'd heard about, Rafael went on to explain.

"It's normal there. Like when you go out to a party, guys wear this thing around their neck. The girls come up to you and…."

"You what? Kiss?" I asked. Honestly, did I really want to know the extent of his romantic escapades?

"Yeah, kind of. It's so common there. Like, it's abnormal if you don't hook up with a lot of girls."

"Really? Even if you don't know each other at all?" Certainly, there was a time when I would have easily stood in judgment and not even given him a chance to explain.

The vagueness in his response left me with little desire to know more. Some things are better left unsaid between a parent and their child. I didn't understand this cultural norm he described. Yet, I accepted it.

After lunch, we stopped by GNC for Rafael to pick up a gigantic container of protein powder, per his request. But before that, we headed to Walmart, also his request. We cruised up and down the aisles as he easily located his beloved Reese's Peanut Butter Cups and Pop-Tarts. Alex and I laughed, watching him revisit these favorite indulgences. Where this gluttonous habit would have once discouraged me, now I knew he was more mature in his lifestyle habits.

"I have to find some chicken. I eat it all the time for protein. Sometimes I even eat it for breakfast. And some fat-free cheese, too."

I observed him in awe as he read labels and mentally computed all the recommended daily serving sizes.

"You know, I realized that the way you suggested is best. If I go too long depriving myself of something, then that's not good. Because you can't do that forever. Because if I relax and let it all go, I go crazy. Like, I really have a problem with food. It's better to do it your way. Find a good balance that's reasonable."

Wow. Who is this young man and what has he done with our Rafael?

That evening, after Frank, Zach, and Emma were home from work, the six of us sat around our farm-style kitchen table for dinner. What a luxury it was, just to pin us down together, given the usual conflicts with everyone's schedules. Strangely, it never dawned on me that prior to Rafael living with us, the chair to my immediate left was always vacant. The five of us had our usual spots, and when Rafael joined our family, he took the remaining chair.

After we finished our spaghetti, I left the table to secretly light the candles on Rafael's dulce de leche cheesecake. Emma discreetly videotaped the scene from a phone and we all began singing "Happy Birthday" as I entered the kitchen.

"Wait, whose birthday is it?" Rafael asked.

"It's for you! We're celebrating your birthday now!" we explained.

I set the cake on the table before him and we encouraged him to blow out the candles. I retrieved his gifts from the dining room table and suggested he unwrap them in between bites of cheesecake. Each gift was numbered, indicating a specific order to proceed. It was a method I used with our kids to heighten the gradual anticipation of the later gifts. Early on in parenting, I learned that once a kid received THAT prized gift, all else paled in comparison.

Attached to each gift was a poetic clue—another Overly tradition—a simple, four-line stanza. The clue forced the recipient to read and speculate as to what the gift was. During Rafael's exchange year, he had witnessed this ritual for all five of our birthdays since they fell between November and April. He, himself, never had the honor of being on the receiving end.

This time, three years after the conclusion of his exchange program, Rafael was celebrated as one of us. It was a different inclusion into our family; he was bestowed the main role in one of our longest-standing traditions.

This was the first summer Alex, Zach, and Emma all had jobs. Initially, I wondered if Rafael would regret visiting since spending time with them was his highlight. Despite this, he seemed satisfied sleeping in, running errands with me, and being my gym buddy. We palled around, easily occupying our time until one or all of the kids could join us. He rode shotgun on our daily outings, with no apparent second thought or hesitancy. We conversed naturally, and perhaps more than what would normally be spoken between most adults and their teenager. Even when there was silence, it was comfortable.

"I never used to talk that much," Rafael described. "I wasn't used to it. But I've been trying to do better. I think talking about things is good."

"Well, you know me. I think communication is healthy. I think that's why we have a really good relationship now. Because we talked about things. We tried to figure things out, especially when there were challenges," I added.

"Yeah, I don't know what I was thinking about back then. Like, why I did certain things or why I didn't. I was stu…born—is that how you say it?"

I chuckled. "Yeah, you were. Stubborn. Remember the donut thing?" I refreshed his mind. "But, you know, you were young. You were fifteen. That's Emma's age now." I couldn't fathom how Emma would cope in an exchange situation at this time. Unless, of course, a host family was seeking sugar and spice in the form of an occasional PMS-ing, stair-stomping, door-slamming teenage girl.

During our many car rides together, Rafael and I shared various introspections about the past, present, and future. I admitted to my crossroads in life, the current one being that I needed to redefine my own path now that Alex, Zach, and Emma were transitioning into independent, young adults. My daily maternal role was waning. Rafael also reflected about what lay ahead in his future.

"I want to talk to Dad sometime," he casually mentioned.

"Oh. About what?" I inquired.

"Like what medical training involves here, in the US," Rafael clarified. "Do you know how the system works? I'm thinking of maybe applying for residency in the States."

I explained the process to him as I remembered it, thinking back to Frank's evolving career when he and I were a young, twenty-something couple. Medical school at the University of Rochester. Pediatric residency at the University of Pittsburgh. Fellowship in emergency medicine at Hasbro Children's Hospital in Providence.

Through the early parts of it, I worked as a physical therapist. But once we had kids, financially, it made sense for me to stay home rather than pay for childcare, but more importantly, I wanted to be our kids' primary caregiver. If I continued working, we would have been two ships passing in the night. I remember Frank's medical training dictating our schedule—and his availability to us—and many days of his absence blurred into nights during which I parented alone. At times it was isolating, but I valued being a constant presence in my kids' lives. Surely other professions and families had it worse, and so we navigated the demands of those years to the best of our ability. It was what worked for us, and it was all we knew.

"You should definitely talk to Dad about it, he can tell you more. It is a long process. Maybe you can even apply to Brown University, but it depends on what you want to specialize in," I baited him, wondering if returning to New England would be a consideration.

"Yeah, that would be good. I'd like that," Rafael claimed.

Part of Rafael's visit included shopping for family and friends. One of them wanted Rafael to buy him clothes and shoes. Rafael also wanted to purchase gifts for Juliana and his family, as a thoughtful offering. Whenever we made Walmy runs, Rafael was right there. He was aware. He was helpful. Whether it was carrying our bagged purchases or loading and unloading things into and out of the car, he initiated the task without being asked. Outside of shopping, he helped unload the dishwasher and hand-washed his own dishes after preparing his chicken breakfasts. Rafael displayed much more insight and consciousness of others. He was a wonder, three years out from his exchange. Like a butterfly breaking out of its cocoon.

"Rafael, I really have to say, you are so different than you used to be. More mature, more helpful," I commended.

"Really? You think so?"

Realizing my comment could be misinterpreted as a backhanded compliment, but truly not meant as such, I recalled our first-year experiences when I frequently asked him to contribute in family chores. Whether it was setting the table, clearing the table, or taking out the garbage, my desire for all my children has always been simply to initiate. *If you don't know what you can do to help, ask.* Thought and awareness score big points in my book. And since I try to praise anyone's efforts, a definite absence from my own childhood, I thought Rafael would appreciate my recognition and feedback.

"Definitely. You're more thoughtful now," I acknowledged. Had this been nature vs. nurture at play? Probably both, but my vote tips the scale on the nurture side. *Wink.*

On one of his last nights with us, after speaking with Frank, Rafael asked me to help him order something on Amazon Prime. It was the first in a series of USMLE books to prepare medical students to sit for a progression of licensing exams. *Boy, he's serious about this residency thing in the US.*

"I have an idea now how to schedule my time and what I need to do when—to study for these exams," he confidently stated, once receiving the book two days later. If once upon a time I ever doubted this kid and his abilities, he made me a believer. Even Frank was pleasantly surprised. So much so that he offered to write Rafael a recommendation letter.

Moral of the story, Rafael showed us life through a different lens. He taught us invaluable lessons, and he proved us wrong in our predictions and misgivings about how his future would unfold. Sure, our exchange experience may have ended three years ago, but the joy, pride, and affection we have for Rafael continue to grow. Who knows what stories our futures will write together. Who knows where the road will take us. With newly open eyes, I can't wait to see.

RAFAEL

(amended slightly for fluidity)

I believe that everyone who's reading this already has a good idea of who I am, but I'll introduce myself anyway. My name is Rafael. I am nineteen today and I'll write a little bit about my exchange year between 2013 and 2014 when I had just turned fifteen. To be honest, I don't remember exactly what made me want to do the exchange program. Somehow the idea came up, and a year before I signed up, I already knew I wanted to do an exchange program in the United States. Why the US? I wanted to learn English fluently. I had thought about England, but since the US has a lot more cultural proximity with South America, I chose the US, thinking this would make the experience a little less shocking for me. I visited Florida before my exchange but two weeks in Miami and Orlando did not provide an accurate picture of what my exchange year would look like. So, in August of 2013, I arrived in New England feeling quite lost.

A day before my birthday, July 23, I received the news that a host family had chosen me. I remember feeling relieved, since I was afraid of not being chosen in time to travel with the first group of people. My host family seemed to be exactly what I desired, and later I realized they actually were what I desired, despite a few normal issues during the year (almost all of them consequences of my immaturity). The transition was a lot more complex than I expected, but the experience shaped me more than I could imagine.

It's hard to remember the details of my first few days in the US because I was on autopilot. It was raining when I met my family. I'm not sure, but I think I fell asleep in the car before we got home (I was so tired). We had dinner in a really good restaurant and watched a movie that night (I slept during most of it). Everything felt surreal. I couldn't believe I was going to spend the next year in a new place. One of the weirdest, but pleasant, feelings I ever had was when I opened my eyes the next day and the reality finally hit me. I was excited and terrified all at once.

I remember spending most of the time out of the house during the first days, which was nice for me, a kid who used to spend his free time inside his room playing video games. My host family taught me to spend a lot more time out of the house, even if it's just walking around (which I love to do today).

My classes were set to start twenty days after my arrival, so I had a little time to adapt. People at school, in general, were really nice to me and the classes weren't hard, considering I was a foreign student, though it took me a few weeks to adapt and produce decent grades. I regret not taking harder classes because when I went back to Brazil, I went to one of the hardest schools in the country, so it would have helped me to study more.

I believe the period when I evolved the most was during my first semester. I learned to have a different vision of the world and opened my mind up. I learned to take the best out of every situation, even when it's extremely tough. My English improved a lot during that first half of the exchange, and I was adjusting to my host family.

Without a doubt, the hardest period was between December and January. Besides the cold and the eternal darkness for the first time ever, I spent Christmas and New Year's out of my house. Back home, we would wait until midnight to eat on Christmas Eve, then we'd swim in the pool and stay up late. I remember staying up all alone in my room at the Overly house and waiting for midnight to roll around, wishing Merry Christmas to myself and going to bed. That was the moment I missed home the most.

On the other hand, Christmas Day was a lot more fun than I'm used to. We woke up early to open gifts and, throughout the entire day, we did a lot of fun things. It was one of the best days of the year, and I truly felt like I was part of the family.

A few days after, we traveled to Pennsylvania to visit my host grandparents and spent the New Year there. Everyone treated me extremely well, and we played football and went snow tubing. My host family was going to host me for one semester, which made me a little nervous about the second half of my exchange. I knew it would be almost impossible to find a family as good as theirs. But, at the end of my first semester, they asked me to stay for the rest of the exchange. I was thrilled and relieved. Everyone agreed with the decision, and I spent another semester with my host family.

In February of 2014, we went skiing for a few days. In March, I went to California with other exchange students. In April, we went to Florida to meet my host grandparents again. Those trips helped me cope with the cold and darkness of that long winter, which was the hardest part of the year. Strangely, AFS doesn't like exchange students to travel. They must have a reason for that, but I'm not sure why.

In May, after much time trying to convince AFS to allow it, my sister and my parents were finally able to visit. My life in the US and my life in Paraguay are two different worlds. It was weird to have them overlap. Even though AFS discourages this kind of visit, I don't see how it could have been negative. I ended up spending more time than recommended with my parents, which caused a few problems with AFS and my host family and, if I think rationally today, I can see why. I'd have my entire life to spend with my real family, but my exchange year was a unique experience, meant to be lived out to the fullest. But it's hard to think like that when you're away from home for nearly a year.

After that, time flew. May and June passed, and it was almost time to go home. I was excited to see everyone, but I didn't want to leave my life and my American family behind. The last day of school was complicated. I distinctly remember looking around and realizing that I wouldn't see 99 percent of my classmates again.

During my final week, I spent every last minute with my host family. We played a lot of basketball, computer games, went to an amusement park, and I even danced a little with my sister (I'm terrible).

Then the day I left came. It was in the beginning of the summer and the day was really hot. I was wearing pants, a polo and boots, because I couldn't fit them in my luggage (that was unpleasant). I usually don't have a hard time saying goodbyes. For that reason, saying goodbye was a little easier than I expected. It didn't seem I was going home just like that after almost a year in the US.

Today, I think about the Rafael in 2013 and I realize how immature I was. I said things I wouldn't normally say, I did a lot of things I wouldn't normally do, and I chose not to do things I should have done. I guess this is one of the most important parts of being an exchange student, being able to change the way you think and act. Evolving as a person.

I am very grateful for what this experience has shown me. I'm grateful for everything I've learned, and for all the time I was able to spend with my host family. Each one of them played a significant role in making this exchange special and memorable for me, and I'm forever indebted to them.

A RAFAEL-ISM GLOSSARY

Rafael-isms pertain to English word-and-phrase inventions Rafael coined throughout our year together. He is credited with the majority of expressions, though Alex, Zach, and Emma had a hand in their evolution.

Note certain commonalities:
*adding the suffix "-ation" (e.g., skypation, okation, homation)
*rhyming phrases

Ain't no nothing—means "I am not…"
In my efforts to improve his English, this was Rafael's fun way to tease me—the more negatives the better.
Alex, in jest: "Rash, you're a loser."
Rafael: "I ain't no nothing."

Deingas bleingas/Deingas (exclamation)—Damn!
"Deingas bleingas, we have a test tomorrow!"

Helloli (salutation)—hi/hello

Goodbye like a lemon pie, which evolved into **Lemonation,** shortened to **Lemon**—goodbye

Opa (exclamation)—oops

"Opa, I forgot to do my homework."

Quick like Richard (adjective, adverb), which originated as **Quick like Dick**, which we nipped in the bud pretty darn fast—fast; quickly

"I have to get ready quick like Richard!"

Solidation (adjective, used in a boastful manner)—good; cool

"My workout was solidation."

Skwerl (noun or verb)—Rafael's misspelling of "squirrel," referring to a bowel movement

"I have to skwerl right now."

"That was a satisfying skwerl."

Or even more odd, Rafael referred to having *"skwerl children."*

2 EZ (adjective, used in a boastful manner)—"I got this!"

This was often accompanied with the index & middle fingers displayed in a "V" formation.

"That basketball shot was 2 EZ."

Weurt (noun, verb)—a specific noise or act of making that noise, wherein the actual noise sounds like the word *weurt;* rhymes with "hurt."

Often, the kids would challenge each other to weurt in public as loud as possible.

Many more Rafael-isms exist; these are just a few. Who knows how they all started or for what reason. It was probably a case of kids being kids. Though many would find these meaningless, they crack us up—like our own language, made up from our own stories, that no one else speaks. It is the language of our very own club.

ACKNOWLEDGMENTS

The process of writing a book has never been about "Can I?" Putting my thoughts into words, then onto paper was easy. The question for me has always been, "How do I?" How do I do all the other stuff that goes into creating a cohesive and tangible story? The answer to that question was simple: collaborate with those that possess the knowledge, skill, and desire to help me reach my goal. These are the people who, from near and far, instilled the information, inspiration, and faith that allowed me to plug along. To them: I thank you. Because of them, I present *Exchange*.

Alysa Smith—you put AFS on my radar and told me long ago: "Someday one of your darts will stick."

Jeanine Silversmith—though the words may never have been spoken, from you, I only "heard" the message: "You've got this."

Rafael—you have no idea how much you have expanded my eyes, mind, and heart.

Leslie & Wilton—Rafael is who he is primarily due to you. I remain awed and grateful for entrusting us with his care and for sharing this journey with us.

AFS—your mission is noble, your efforts commendable: spreading good will across borders one family at a time.

Frank—you embrace my many quirks and indulge my kooky ideas with love and laughter. Your support boosts me up and your belief in me never waivers. You cherish me like no other. *How lucky am I?*

Alex, Zach, and Emma—you personify my heart.

Matt Smith—I so appreciate your never-want-to-settle approach to your artistry. Your cover is the sprinkles on an Allie's Donut, the icing on a Rhode Island famous Greggs's cake, and the cherry on top of a Newport Creamery Sundae.

Lisa Cerasoli—you held my hand (remotely) step-by-step, navigating the literary world. You patiently lent your creative and technical expertise to showcase my work. Professionally, you were my editor; personally, you are the friend I have yet to meet.

Exchange

Made in the USA
Middletown, DE
06 May 2019